The diary, notes and sketches compiled
in Lincolnshire in 1840
and in
Wythburn, Cumberland 1849-1852
by Basil Ranaldson Lawson,
Curate and Vicar of Wythburn
1849-1892

Exposition and comment
by
Margaret Armstrong

To Peggy

ISBN 0 9515173 0 9

Printed by Ferguson Bros. (Printers) Ltd., Keswick.
Published by PEEL WYKE PUBLICATIONS
22 Brandlehow Crescent, Keswick, Cumbria, CA12 4JE.

FOREWORD

In 1984, Thirlmere dropped to a very copy of an Ordnance Survey map of 1867, places known to me only from the old Wythburn church registers. This did something to create an impression of the valley of which the Revd. B. R. Lawson was vicar. Imagine my excitement, therefore, on reading this book. Margaret Armstrong has really brought to life the old community of Wythburn, with the aid of the diary and the sketches of Basil Lawson.

I hope that others will experience the same sense of pleasure that I did.

Geoffrey Darrall.
Vicar of St. John's-in-the-Vale and Wythburn.

LIST OF ILLUSTRATIONS

O.S. Map Grid references are given where they are likely to be useful. The prefix NY is not given but applies to all references.

CONTENTS

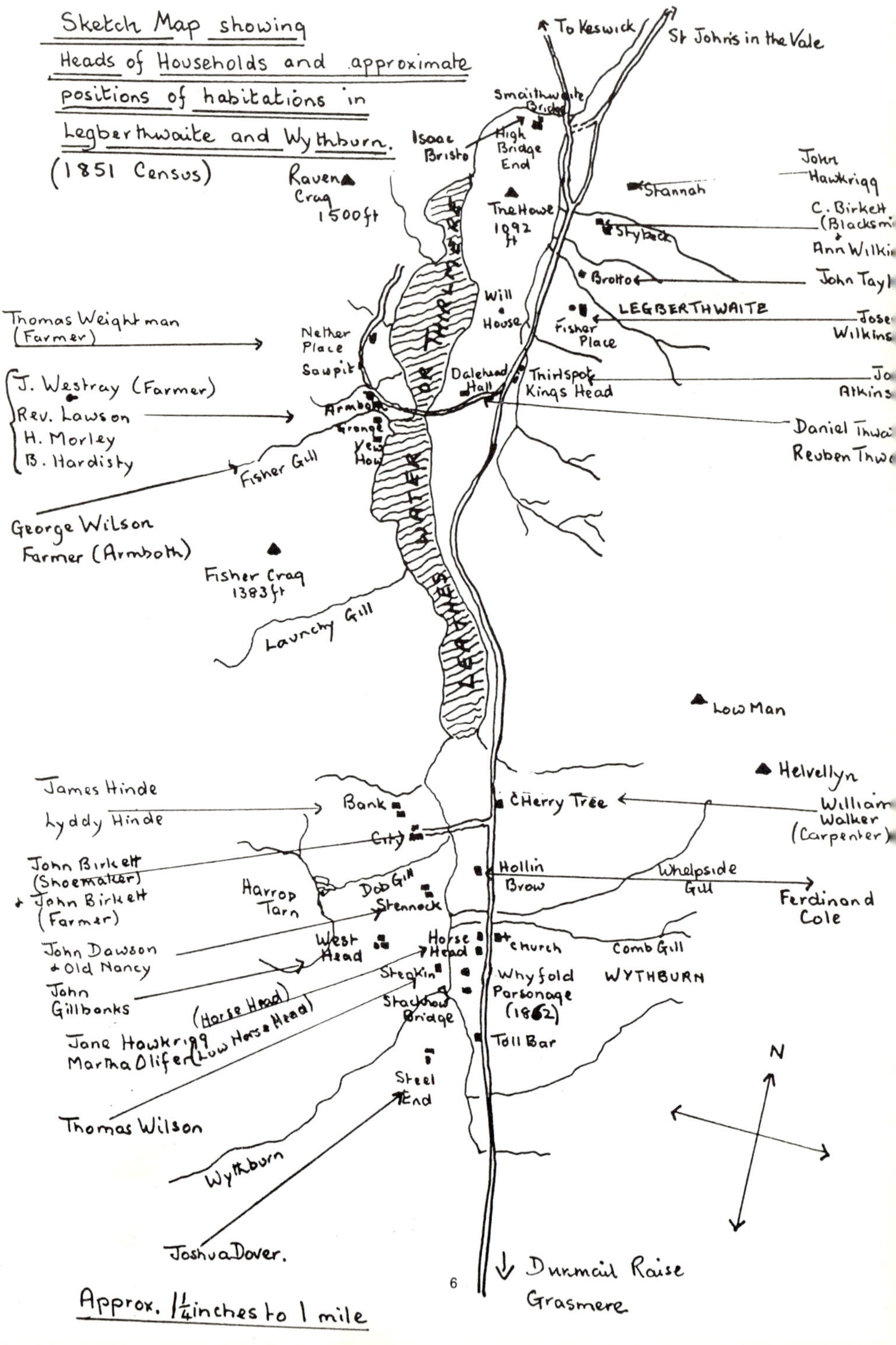
Sketch Map showing
Heads of Households and approximate
positions of habitations in
Legberthwaite and Wythburn.
(1851 Census)
To Keswick
St Johns in the Vale
Smaithwaite Bridge
Isaac Bristo
High Bridge End
Raven Crag 1500ft
The Howe 1092 ft
Stannah
John Hawkrigg
C. Birkett (Blacksmi
& Ann Wilki
Styback
Brotto
John Tayl
Will House
LEGBERTHWAITE
Fisher Place
Jose
Wilkins
Thomas Weightman (Farmer)
Nether Place
Sawpit
THIRLMERE
Dalehead Hall
Thirlspot Kings Head
Jo
Atkins
J. Westray (Farmer)
Rev. Lawson
H. Morley
B. Hardisty
Armboth
Grange
Yew How
Daniel Thwai
Reuben Thw
Fisher Gill
George Wilson Farmer (Armboth)
Fisher Crag 1383ft
LEATHES WATER
Launchy Gill
Low Man
Helvellyn
James Hinde
Lyddy Hinde
Bank
Cherry Tree
William Walker (Carpenter)
City
John Birkett (Shoemaker)
& John Birkett (Farmer)
Harrop Tarn
Dob Gill
Stennock
Hollin Brow
Whelpside Gill
Ferdinand Cole
John Dawson & Old Nancy
West Head
Horse Head
Church
Comb Gill
John Gillbanks
Stegkin
Whyfold
WYTHBURN
Parsonage (1862)
(Horse Head)
(Low Horse Head)
Stackhow Bridge
Jane Hawkrigg
Martha Olifer
Toll Bar
N
Steel End
Thomas Wilson
Wythburn
Joshua Dover.
Dunmail Raise
Grasmere
Approx. 1¼ inches to 1 mile

INTRODUCTION

It is possible, particularly on a frosty morning in spring or autumn, to climb a Lakeland fell side through a swathe of mist and reach a sunlit world where the craggy tops are islands in a milky sea. The warming sun burns and clears the swirling vapours and momentarily a small patch of valley is revealed in detail far below. It is lit briefly by a golden beam before the fog covers it again or it is completely cleared and becomes part of the greater landscape.

Such is the experience that, in terms of time, the 'Little Book of Parson Lawson' reveals. To read his notes from April 1849 until December 1852 is to perceive illuminated those far off days in the Vale of Wythburn when he was meeting inhabitants and visitors, going into homes and sharing activities. The period is brief before the clarity is gone. Much of even the tangible remains are literally covered by the waters, those still there are part of a changed environment.

A small leather covered notebook was found by my friend, Miss Margaret Stanley when she dealt with the property of her brother, Edwin who died in Keswick in 1986. On the front cover was written the name J. (Jonathon) Stanley, their grandfather who was a miller at Wanthwaite in the Vale of St. John. It was obviously not written by him, since he was a child aged three in 1849 and it was not known to whom it had originally belonged.

Knowing of my interest in local history, Miss Stanley showed the little book to me wondering if I could find any clues to the identity of the writer. Study revealed that the owner must have been a local clergyman, that his wife was 'Mrs. L---' and that 'Bazzy' was their child.

A leaflet for visitors to the church of Saint John's in the Vale written by the present Vicar, Reverend C. Geoffrey Darrell, gave a clue that someone with the surname initial 'L' and a son 'Bazzy' or Basil could be Basil R. Lawson, appointed curate of Wythburn Chapelry in 1849. Comparison of various dates and handwriting in the book with entries in the parish registers of Saint John's in the Vale and Wythburn confirmed the theory and from then on the contents became the basis of an absorbing quest to discover more of the man and life in Wythburn before the Waterworks Committee of Manchester set to work on the Thirlmere valley.

Basil Lawson's own words from his last written page proved strangely significant.

"Little books, like little men are often despised by us. But it often happens that little books like little men contain a great deal of valuable information and have more to recommend them than those of larger dimensions. This proceeds from the circumstance of our allowing ourselves to be too much guided by the eye and by appearances. Thus it often happens that in judging of both before we have examined them we are attracted by one on which much expense has been bestowed in the binding a (gild)? of it: whilst we pass by another which has nothing particular externally to attract the Eye but whose modest exterior contains much work and excellence. We judge of books in this respect as we judge of men. A bold and showy exterior imposes on us and we give a man credit for being of more consequence than he really is. Examination proves him to be but tinsel and glitter, a mere bauble. The real Grace is accepted under a common and ordinary outside".

Examining what is contained in the common and ordinary outside I found there a great deal of valuable information, much work and excellence and not a little grace. Secondary sources were used first; all books consulted being listed in the bibliography. Then followed the primary sources, maps, parish records, census returns, contemporary and later newspapers and fieldwork. The latter was invaluable in bringing atmosphere and a sense of place.

Standing outside the whitewashed chapel at Wythburn when the rain of a winter Sunday has dispersed the walkers and discouraged the motorists one can imagine Parson Lawson crossing the old bridge from Armboth to preach to a handful of drenched villagers. On December 19th 1852 he wrote:-
'very wet - Congregation 4!!'
A hamlet in Wythburn, called 'The City' is submerged beneath the raised lake that became Manchester's water supply; Armboth Hall, The Parsonage, School, Inns and farms are all demolished and overgrown but some of the places Parson Lawson wrote about remain. A tumbled wall here, a pavement there, tracks almost lost in the trees, mossed gateposts, all bear witness to the life that once was. A new road has been made, houses have been built for the Waterworks staff but due to the scheme much is as Parson Lawson knew it. Had this not gone forward and there was much opposition at the time, the valley would probably have been subjected to the same sort of development as that seen on the outskirts of Keswick at Braithwaite and Portinscale. Lead mining which might have caused despoilation as elsewhere ceased as the dam was built and the water began to flow southward. The marginal planting of conifers was and still is controversial but until recently the public was denied access to the risen lake preventing damage by car wheels and erosion from the tread of tourists.

Supplementing, the script, I tried to add explanation and facts of interest for local historians and others who live in or visit the area but most of all I have endeavoured to portray the man mentioned by Canon Rawnsley as 'Honoured by and an honour to the parish which he served'.

While carrying out my research, I traced and in March 1989 had the great pleasure of meeting, ninety-five year old Miss Ada Ranaldson Hallam, only child of the Reverend Lawson's youngest daughter. Interested in and pleased with the work that I had already done, she gave to me her grandfather's sketch books and family photograph album thus adding an extra and exciting dimension to my study.

Where comment and guesswork are involved this is entirely my own responsibility as are errors and omissions.

ACKNOWLEDGEMENTS

The author wishes to acknowledge the help given over three years by the Cumbria Archive Service at Carlisle and Kendal, especially Mrs. Susan Dench, the County Library Services at Carlisle and Kendal, Mr. W. Elsby and his staff at Keswick Library, Lincolnshire and Leicestershire County Record Services, Dr. Carol Landon, Mr. and Mrs. G. Hindmoor of Matterdale, Mr. John Airey of Keswick and the Rev. C. G. Darrell, Vicar of St. John's in the Vale, Wythburn and Legberthwaite. Special thanks are due to Miss M. Stanley, who found the 'Little Book', to Miss Ada Hallam for her interest and gifts of illustrative material, to Mr. George Bott of Keswick for constructive suggestions after reading the typescript and to my husband Harold for continuous patience and encouragement, also sincere thanks for the interest and professional expertise of the printers Ferguson Bros. of Keswick.

Keswick. 1989

NURTURE OF A NORTH COUNTRY PARSON

Basil Ranaldson Lawson, the fifth son of the Reverend Dr. George Lawson, Vicar of Heversham, Westmorland and his wife Henrietta Ranaldson of Blair Athol, was baptised on the 1st June 1807.

It would appear that Basil's early years were spent in an unconventional household. Dr. George Lawson, formerly a Fellow of Trinity College, Cambridge became Vicar of Heversham in 1797. Within a few years arrangements were being made to obtain an enclosure Act for the area. The owners of four fifths of the land had to agree before this could take place. The Honourable Mary Howard of Levens Hall disputed with Dr. Lawson as negotiations progressed, beginning a quarrel with him which lasted for forty years.

In anticipation of the reapportionment of land and evidently hoping to embark on large scale farming the Vicar obtained plots for himself and his brother. The venture failed and they ran into debt. Dr. Lawson borrowed money which he could not pay back and at one time had the Bailiffs in the house. He was discredited amongst some of his parishioners and his churchwardens refused to give him a reference when he sought to augment his income by teaching at Heversham School.

The Enclosure Act received the Royal Assent just before the Battle of Waterloo and later that year Dr. Lawson planted the chestnut trees which still stand in the churchyard. It is thought that he did this as much in the relief at the clearance of some debts as in celebration of the victory. Young Basil, eight or nine years old could have witnessed the planting.

The Reverend Dr. George Lawson must subsequently have regained his reputation as his memorial high up on the north wall of the sanctuary of Heversham Church, records on a scroll of white on black marble that it was 'Placed there by his parishioners in affectionate remembrance'. He died on June 14th 1842 and had been Vicar for upwards of forty years. On the scroll is a somewhat cryptic inscription.

'The blessing of him that was ready to perish came upon him; and he caused the widows heart to sing with joy'.

A family memory says that Rev. Dr. George Lawson was an M.A. and M.D. not a D.D. and doctored all the poor people his his parish.

In the churchyard a prominent memorial marks the Lawson family's grave. A plinth of rough stone over a yard square supports four triangular slate slabs and a capping stone. One slab bears the words 'Behind this cold memorial lie the remains of Henrietta Lawson, as a wife and mother affectionate and to the needy bountiful'. She died in 1825 when Basil would be nineteen. Another slab records the life of his sister Tamar, who according the the Census was with her father at Heversham vicarage in 1841. She lived to be eighty-seven and was killed in France in 1888.

It is reasonable to surmise that Basil R. Lawson was educated at Heversham School but no evidence of his activities appear until the 1830's when he was studying at St. Bees College and according to Crockford's Clerical Directory was ordained priest by the Bishop of Chester in 1838. The theological college at St. Bees was founded in 1816 by Bishop Law of Chester. It was an alternative to the universities of Oxford and Cambridge as a way of obtaining entrance to Holy Orders. Basil Lawson as a younger son of less than affluent parents was probably glad to take advantage of the high standard offered by his diocesan college. A. G. Bradley, writing in 1901 mentions St. Bees as famous and 'a prolific nursery of

Arn both Sawpit.

Old Horses Cote
nr Wyth Burn.

Sep 17.

north country parsons', adding that it was also somewhat invidiously known as a back door into the Anglican Church.

A LINCOLNSHIRE NOTEBOOK

The little brown notebook appears to have originated in Lincolnshire since a map of the county is printed on the inner front cover and from 1840 begins to tell its own story. Most of the pages are taken up with a diary, which may be of interest to meteorologists as it records the Cumbrian weather from 1849 - 1852, along with notes of people and events that concerned the Parson sufficiently for him to write about them. There are also several pages of prose, including an extract from one of his own sermons. Pencil sketches show scenes around Thirlmere, a young man with a churchwarden pipe and the head of an aged man. There is some doggerel verse and small drawings of hounds, a hurrying man and a cat which may have been done to amuse the child 'Bazzy'. Scribble over them suggests that he was not impressed.

Material on the first page suggests that the Reverend Basil Lawson was connected with a gaol and enquiries have revealed that he served as a curate to the parish of Spalding between the years 1838 and 1843 and is likely also to have acted as chaplain to the Spalding House of Correction.

'August 1840 8th, 12th, 19th (very bad temper)
25th much improved pleaded indisposition and infirmity.'

Then comes a list of names 'Messrs. Chambers 19th
Turner 19th
Turnbull 18th
Allan Betts 19th'

Beside these names, indistinctly in pencil 'a word in season on preparation for death. Thus preparation for eternity. Bp. Patrick's persuasive proofs a cheerful perseverance and trust in God'.

Perhaps these named persons were under sentence of death and the newly ordained curate was called upon to minister to them.

Also on this page is a list of twenty three diocese with their bishops. Maybe application to some of these would provide an avenue of escape from a situation not altogether congenial.

A tiny pencilled note following the 'Gaol' material indicated more bad temper. 'The vile places of South Holland - Gedney, Whaplode, Drove and Crowland'

Further notes record that the Rev. Lawson ordered spelling books, prayer books and Bibles for the Gaol use. Dates of visiting are entered with some comment.

'Aug 1st
1840 Gaol - prisoners Male 25 female 7
Sep 30th - visited - a rough set waiting for trial charged with felony
The old tale innocence mixed up with charges of perjury and malignity on the part of their prosecutors - & with protestations of amendment.
Little good to be done I doubt.
an ill arranged tho' well conducted gaol for instance no apartment exclusively set apart for debtors - but are mixed with deserters, imbeciles and others.
Nov 2nd - a thoughtless set convicted of riot at Gedney.
10th - found the prisoners willing to instruct each other.
28th - find them more attentive & respectful.

Dec 30th - have come to the resolution that it is nothing but a matter of prose to record in order and succession visits to the gaol - nevertheless visited. Feb 2nd 5th 8th - am certain of this that no man can make a silken purse out of a sow's lug.

Resignation and acceptance seem to have replaced the bad temper as this period of apprenticeship to his calling comes to an end.

There are now six years during which traces are scant but in 1845 Basil R. Lawson was the officiating minister at a marriage at Market Bosworth, Leicestershire but not apparently either rector or curate there. He evidently married in Leicestershire and the baptism register for Barlestone records that Basil Ranaldson Lawson son of Basil Ranaldson Lawson, clerk of Osbaston in the parish of Market Bosworth and his wife Elizabeth Ann was baptised privately by his father 28th February 1848.

Parson Lawson may have been ministering in various places. Many clergymen at this time were incumbents of several parishes, often considerable distances apart. They employed others without specific appointments to officiate for them.

RETURN TO THE NORTH

By February 1849 Parson Lawson was back in his native Westmorland, at Grasmere and in March came over the Raise into Legberthwaite, Cumberland. With his wife and son he took rooms with a Mrs. Westray of the King's Head at Thirlspot and wrote in the little book the first impressions of his surroundings. Immediately there is conveyed a sense of satisfaction and tranquillity: an interest in wildlife, local history and a concern for those with whom he comes into contact is clear. Appreciation of a calm evening and accounts of storm and tempest will surprise no modern day dweller in this area where changing weather ever dominates activities.

Daily notes of weather and the curate's pattern of life begin April 1849 and the little book is filled up by December 1852. It is interesting to speculate on the continuance of the diary habit and wonder if somewhere more notebooks exist. The Reverend Basil R. Lawson is gradually revealed in his own words as a most likeable man. At first he looks around him, makes natural observations, is whimsical about ducks and cynical about tourists. He hears from friends in Leicestershire and Lincolnshire and begins to meet local people and visitors. He enjoys walking on Helvellyn, fishing the becks and being 'out with the dogs' hunting the fox. Family and chapel life, friends to tea, farming matters and a little gossip occupy his days with only brief excursions and indications of the world beyond Wythburn. He is accepted and on the way to becoming the 'Good Shepherd of his flock' as Canon Rawnsley described him.

But this serenity, this self-contained security lasted little more than twenty years. In the 1870's Reverend Lawson as Vicar, now, of Wythburn learned with the people of the Vale of Thirlmere, that their whole way of life was to be changed for ever as the scheme for providing an abundance of pure water for the City of Manchester was set in motion.

As Parson Lawson took up the threads of his daily life in Wythburn, he could have had no idea of what would come to pass, but he would have had more knowledge of the heritage into which he had entered. William Wordsworth in his 'Guide to the District of the Lakes' published in 1835 describes the gradual settlement of the more 'secluded valleys' and the establishment of chapels which in their turn became 'mother churches to smaller edifices planted at length in almost every dale throughout the country.'

Crosthwaite Church, Keswick, an early foundation dedicated to the Celtic Saint Kentigern was the mother church of the chapelries of Borrowdale, Newlands, Braithwaite, Saint John's in the Vale and Wythburn. These daughter churches were all established in the 16th century as the changes in the English social order begun by the dissolution of the monasteries and hastened by the inflation of Elizabeth the 1st's reign began to take effect. Around Keswick it is likely that improving prosperity consequent on the demand for farming produce, a healthy market and the development of mining interests caused an increase of the population there and in the outlying areas and thus a need for places of worship and the services of curates.

Saint John's in the Vale and Wythburn were consecrated in 1554. At Saint John's it is probably that an earlier chapel had existed as it stands on the route of a medieval trackway from the west to Matterdale and Penrith. There is evidence of a building at Wythburn by 1640 but the chapel that Parson Lawson came to had been rebuilt in 1740. It was a simple rectangular structure with thick stone walls and a stone flagged floor.

In 'Excursion VII' Wordsworth describes the arrival of a priest coming over rough tracks to a small chapel, his goods and children in panniers on the backs of pack-horses. This was supposedly the Reverend Joseph Simpson a former parson of Wythburn often mentioned in Dorothy Wordsworth's Journal.

When he travelled north from Leicestershire the Reverend Lawson and his family are likely to have used the new railway which reached Windermere in 1847 and there was a regular coach service over Dunmail Raise.

The Bishop of the Diocese of Carlisle when Reverend Lawson took up his curacy was Hugh Percy. His name is noted on the first page of the Little brown notebook but otherwise is not mentioned. He was succeeded in 1856 by Bishop Henry Montague Villiers who was energetic in diocesan reorganisation, using the railway system to visit churches and chapels. He took action on the long standing matter of the incorporation of certain parts of Cumberland and Westmorland which were in Chester diocese into that of Carlisle. A Commissioners report of 1836 had proposed these changes and an Order in Council of 1847 authorised the addition of 49 parishes including St. Bees and Heversham. However Bishop Percy refused his permission and this did not take place until his death. Even so, when the Reverend Basil R. Lawson was appointed to Wythburn in 1849 the scene would be set for change.

In 1835 one half of the benefices of the Carlisle diocese were held in plurality. A well-connected clergyman could be the incumbent of several parishes, live the life of a country gentleman and become quite wealthy while employing poorly paid curates to act for him. Reforming acts of 1836 and 1840 set out to redistribute the wealth of the church and improve the stipends of the poorer parsons and curates: payment of a rent charge instead of a rendering of tithes in kind had removed a grievance often held against the clergy generally. Parson Lawson could hope for a welcome from his parishioners. True, one hundred years earlier John Wesley had noted that 'Cumberland people were imbued with the idea that priests should work at their trade for wages, like any other men'. These wages were still likely to be meagre. According to C. M. L. Bouch in 'Prelates and People of the lake Counties.' the average annual stipend in the

Carlisle diocese was £175 in 1835, whereas in the whole of England and Wales it was £285. It was not just financial considerations which called Parson Lawson back from the Midlands. The living of Wythburn was worth £82 p.a. in 1847.

The Vicar of Crosthwaite, patron of the living of Wythburn and thus of Parson Lawson was the Reverend James Lynn. At Saint John's in the Vale the Reverend Edward Wilson was the incumbent for whom the Reverend James Bush junior officiated. At Wythburn the incumbent was Isaac Denton. Officiating for him was the Reverend James Bush senior and it was after his death in 1849 that Reverend Basil Lawson came to take his place. The Reverends Bush, senior and junior had rooms at Dalehead Hall owned by Thomas Leathes Stanger Leathes, Lord of the Manor of Legberthwaite, but the Lawson family went first to a humbler abode the King's Head at Thirlspot. The landlady was Jane Westray, a widow who with her son, also farmed 69 acres of arable, meadow and pasture land.

What of the other parishioners? The 1841 census figures have for St. John's, Wythburn, Armboth, Legberthwaite and Smeathwaite 191 persons, 96 male and 95 95 female in 34 habitations plus 7 uninhabited dwellings. Occupations listed for the heads of households show that there were 10 farmers, 3 carpenters, 2 stonemasons, 2 blacksmiths, a waller, a miller, 1 joiner, a shoemaker, a publican (Jane Westray) and a tea dealer. One person was in the army and three had independent means. The enumerator, Richard Knubley, listed no increase or decrease in the population since the last census so it can be surmised that these persons together with farm servants, house servants, housewives and scholars maintained a stable self-contained life style based upon agriculture.

Occupations are predominantly the same in 1851 when that census records 203 persons, 108 male and 95 female in 38 habitations. There were then 5 uninhabited dwellings in the same area. There was an additional Inn-Keeper, Jane Hawkrigg at the Horse Head and John Atkinson was now the landlord at Thirlspot. Mrs. Westray had crossed the lake to Armboth with farmer son, Joseph. Parson Lawson and his family had gone with them, as lodgers.

Also recorded in 1851 are, a Toll bar keeper, a schoolmaster, two lead miners, a visitor and a groom. John Atkinson of the King's Head, born in Lancashire had married a local girl and with the lead miners and the visitor indicate the slow infiltration of outsiders to the valley. Alex McFadzean in his book on the Wythburn Mine describes the influx of miners following the discovery of an outcropping mineral vein on the flank of Helvellyn Low Man and the consequent development of the mine Wheal Henry in the 1840's. There were more miners in the north-east section of St. John's in the Vale, including Fernside, Wanthwaite, Burns Quarter and Goosewell, which had slightly more population, 196 persons, 108 males and 88 females. Parson Lawson would have contact with these people when he officiated at St. John's since there were no burials or marriages at Wythburn then.

These few incomers were the first to invade the valley since the landowners and farmers had become settled. Hundreds of workmen would come as the Manchester Waterworks Scheme was undertaken. The one listed visitor was the forerunner of millions.

By the middle of the 19th century the middle classes had discovered the Lake District. Many families from the industrial areas had enough money to take a house for the summer, lodge in farmhouses or stay in the new boarding houses and hotels. Railways provided easy transport over long distances and wagonettes met them at the stations. Guidebooks were being produced urging the whole of Britain to get to know the Lake District and it became fashionable. Costs were set out as no doubt those who had worked hard to make the new holidays possible looked for value for their money as they spent it.

In early guide books the inn, The Horse Head, later called the Nag's Head at Wythburn is often recommended as one of the starting points for ascending Helvellyn or as a place for refreshment after descent. It was 'a nice clean little inn' according to Harriet Martineau. Parson Lawson would meet with these tourists and some of the names in his diary not traceable to local people may refer to visitors lodging at Legberthwaite and Armboth. He would be the obvious person to ask about lore and tradition. Soon after his arrival he notes culled tales of floods including the story of the great storm of 1749 when the mill at Legberthwaite and a kiln were washed away in five minutes and the millstones never again found. Cottages were crushed and swept away and the terrified inhabitants climbed trees and clambered on to the tops of haystacks. There must have been many wild storms before and since, including some recorded by Parson Lawson himself but this had to be exceptional for the memories to be handed down for a hundred years. The printed tale appeared in a Gentleman's Magazine of 1754 and again in William Hutchinson's History of the County of Cumberland first published in the 1790's. It has been promulgated in directories and countless volumes on the Lake District with more or less accuracy ever since.

Parson Lawson's sketch of the Kings Head, Legberthwaite.

Apart from the development of one mine, the Thirlmere valley remained as it was in 1849 when Parson Lawson took up his duties until the coming of the workers of the Manchester Waterworks scheme in the 1880's. On the Tithe map of 1847 Leathes Water is the name of the narrow lake some 2½ to 3 miles long, nipped and bridged near the centre between the west promontory at Armboth and the east promontory below Dalehead Hall. Old drawings show a varied appearance for the bridge.

It had several stone piers connected by a wooden walkway and rails. The water would flow between the piers and the wooden structure could easily be replaced after wind and flood damage. On Christmas Day 1852, writes Parson Lawson, it was blown away in a terrific storm.

Small fields bounded by stone walls fringed the lakehead and waterside and were planted with oats, potatoes and carrots. The meadows provided hay and grazing land. Almost all are now under water but even in unsubmerged valleys similar to Thirlmere of old, this pattern of cultivation has disappeared. There is ample evidence in his diary that once settled at Wythburn the new curate observed and even played his part in the daily round of farming life. He mentions sewing and reaping, sheep washing and clipping and cutting peats. Perhaps he inherited his fathers dreams of owning and managing land, however there is no indication that he kept flocks of his own sheep as did a former Wythburn curate William Sewell about whose exploits there many anecdotes in William Dickinson's 'Cumbriana'.

SETTLING IN

Parson Lawson's diary from April 1849 shows the normal reaction of anyone taking up residence and occupation in a new location. Friendships and involvement come only gradually. For over a year even references to his ministry are sparse until in June 1850 he begins to record the weekly attendances at chapel. His first concern is with the weather and the physical world around him. From the entries April to August 1849 come delightful observations in phrases suggesting a gentle and receptive mind.

'Silky clouds hang over Saddleback'

'Evening clouds, lower than the Armboth fells, slowly creeping along. Went on the How, mild as midsummer tho there was a thin cloud of snow enveloping me passing away to the south into Grasmere.'

'at night stars shone brightly as seen from my sleeping room window - at 3 stars gone and the sky cloudy. It has rained since five.'

'evening sky feathery and ragged'

Later the weather observations are curtailed to fine, warm, cloudy, wet or stormy with few descriptive adjectives.

One simple sentence on 15th May surely gives a clue to the nature of the man.

planted one little potato which I found in ye road.'

Parson Lawson was also a man prepared to listen and he devoted a page of his notebook to the first tales that were told to him.

Local traditions. Amongst these is to ~~be~~ be mentioned the ~~the~~ history of the Wey foot, (Whey foot) Stone in Borrodale. Tradition says that it took its name from the circumstance of a man stealing a calf or Whey Calf, during snow & who in order to prevent the calf being traced carried it on his Shoulders; but becoming tired put the calf down on the road, when the Evil one imprinted the calf's foot on the Stone, which led to detection. It is not far from the Bolder Stone. – D. Thwaite.

Early in the last Century, one of the Leathes' family of Dalehead lodged at the old House at Armboth with the Mother of the late Wilson Jackson. Mr Leathes paid for the maintenance of himself horse & dog – £7 – per ann & considered that he paid liberally. The original road from Keswick passed thro' Armboth, under Raven Crag – & so to Amblende under the ~~Pearson~~ Fisher Crag and so to Wythburn. At that period all family and household matters were managed in a primitive way. The tailor, Shoemaker, blacksmith &c all attending at the house when wanted, and remaining until the family were supplied for the Season.

The high road from Keswick to Amblende afterwards left the Armboth side of the lake, and passed thro' Dalehead Hall field to the Wally House under the Great Howe, which Wally house was at that time a Public. The whole traffic was conveyed on Pack horses. The traffic must have been considerable as there were three public houses at that time in Wythburn – Waterhead house, Cherrytree, and the present Inn. John Hawes's father remembered the present road from Wythburn to Keswick being made. The two bridges between the Brow and Stone Head in Wythburn, which are still standing & in use were old bridges at that time. Gray in his tour seems to contradict this, when he speaks of the road in his day (1769) & passing over the Park Brow in Leg northwards.

Actual Size

Transcription of this page with my notes.

Local traditions. Amongst these is to be mentioned the history of the Way foot (whey foot) stone in Borrowdale. Tradition says that it takes its name from the circumstance of a man stealing a calf or whey calf, during snow and who in order to prevent the calf being traced carried it on his shoulders; but becoming tired put the calf down on the road, when the evil one imprinted the calf's foot on the stone, which led to detection. It is not far from the Bolder Stone. D. Thwaite. (Note: Evidently told to Parson Lawson by Daniel Thwaite who was a farmer at Dalehead.)

Early in the last century, one of the Leathes family of Dalehead lodged at the old House at Armboth with the mother of the late Wilson Jackson. Mr. Leathes paid for the maintenance of himself, horse and dog £7 pr ann, and considered that he paid liberally.
(Note; probably from Adam Wilkinson manservant to Wilson Jackson. Jackson was 85 in 1841 census and died before Rev. Lawson came to Wythburn. The family had been dalesmen at Armboth for a long period and also had connections with the silk trade in London according to Harwood's History of the Thirlmere Waterworks Scheme. 1895.)

The road from Keswick passed thro' Armboth, Under Raven Crag and so to Ambleside under the Fisher Crag and to Wythburn. At that period all family and household matters were arranged in a primitive way: the tailor, shoemaker, blacksmith etc. All attending at the house when wanted and remaining until the family were supplied for the season.

The high road from Keswick to Ambleside afterwards left the Armboth side of the lake, and passed thro' Dalehead Hall field to the Willy House under the Great Howe, which Willy house was at that time a *Public.* The whole traffic was conveyed on Pack horses. The traffic must have been considerable as there were *three public* houses at that time in Wythburn, Waterhead House, Cherry Tree and the present Inn. John Hinde's father remembered the present road from Wythburn to Keswick being made. The *two bridges* between the Brow and Horse Head in Wythburn, which are still standing and in use were old bridges at that time.

Gray in his tour seems to contradict this: when he speaks of the road in his day (1769) passing over Park Brow in Legberthwaite.

(Note: Willy House is shown on the first Ordnance Survey Maps as Will House. John Hinde was the widower schoolmaster living in 1851 (Census) with his brother James, a farmer, at Bank just NW of City. Parson Lawson was to bury them both, James in 1863 and John in 1870.

The two bridges were over Whelpside Gill and Comb Gill, now they are gone and the becks are discreetly culverted under the tarmaced road.)

Horse Head Inn, Chapel and Low Horse Head, Wythburn from the West.

From 1847 Tithe Map

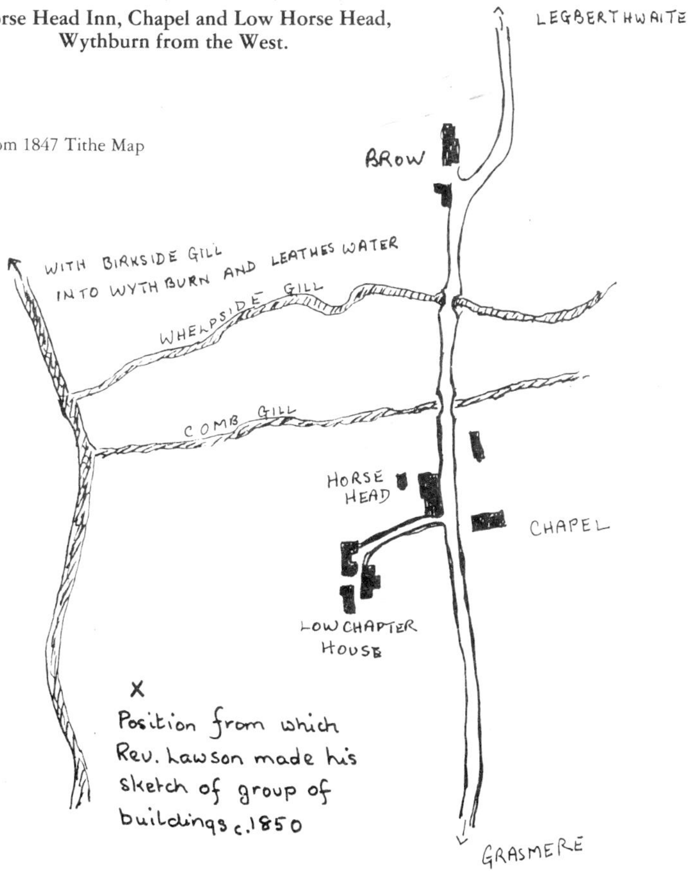

Dalehead Hall from Legberthwaite, Armboth Fells in the distance.

THE TOURISTS

For over a year after coming to Wythburn Parson Lawson was intrigued by the tourists. On April 6th 1849 he noted a 'Party on Helvellyn. Kendal Bumps.' Kendal bump was a term for a rough type of yarn made from the wool of black faced sheep. The 19th Century knitters of the dales used it to make coarse stockings, jerseys and caps when the trade for good quality hand knitted hosiery made from worsted had slumped. (Dr. J. Satchell. Kendal on Tenterhooks.)

Was the Parson referring then, to the garments worn for walking or using a scoffing term applied by someone who was raised just outside the town, to the people of Kendal? Mr. J. Hughes of Kendal tells me that as youths, he and his friends referred to the lads from across the river at Farcross as 'Kendal bumpers'. It was definitely a term of derision applied by youngsters to someone from a less socially desirable area, as youngsters will, but he has no idea why they were so called.

On the 10th April, Parson Lawson has sympathy with two tourists battling against the wind when he says they 'attempted to ascend Helvellyn. Had to give up could not stand'. On 30th April, the day after Easter Sunday he ascended Helvellyn himself. He found it warm with a gentle breeze but the sun created a murky atmosphere so that he could not enjoy any distant view. He fancied that no one had been there before him that year but beside this, either he or someone else has written faintly 'humbug Basil'. This entry finishes:- 'A party was up on Good Friday - snobs of course'.

Early in May a gentleman arrived from Lincolnshire having been lost on Whiteside above the King's Head. He presumably stayed the night and struck up an acquaintance, based on talk of Lincolnshire where Parson Lawson had lived for several years. The next day he accompanied the gentleman into Borrowdale, thence to Keswick and returned for dinner. Quite a ride!

A week later 'Tourists increase, spavined, wind galled and sure-footed.' Spavined is a word usually applicable to a swollen hock joint in a horse, so the parson could be referring to the tourists or their ponies. Wind galled would be chafed by the wind.

By May 11th he is using gently humorous ornithological similies. 'The wild weather has stopped the flight of the tourists. Have not seen any for two days. They are a summer bird; not found in White nor mentioned by Ray'.

Finally for that year on May 15th 'Tourists have vanished. Those who came must have carried a discouragement back with them'.

It was an erroneous supposition for in the Cumberland Pacquet of Tuesday July 24th 1849 under Local Intelligence, is this report:-

> 'We are glad to learn that Keswick and the Lake District in general continue to be well filled with visitors who seem well charmed with the scenery of Cumberland and Westmorland and delighted with the hospitality of our mountaineers and dalesmen; so superior to the mercenary welcome of the Rheinlanders and the ill favoured Swiss whose uncouth manners, unsavoury dishes, inconvenient regulations for travelling and exorbitant charges nothing could have rendered tolerable but fashion which we now trust is setting in a more homely direction.'

The writer is obviously welcoming as is Parson Lawson who soon becomes accustomed to the visitors. They cease to be in his mind when he jots things down. He makes only two more entries concerning them. On Easter Sunday 1850 there are 'A few Easter tourists on the road'.

But, so pleased is he on June 9th that he emphasises 'good congregation 56 - few tourists hitherto'.

Fisher Houses from The Howe, Legburthwaite 1849

Stack How Bridge, Wythburn.
Remains can be seen near Steel End car park.

Farm House at Armboth - demolished.

BIRDS, FISH AND FOXES

That the Reverend Basil Lawson took a delight in all creatures great and small is conveyed by many lines in his diary. In mid April 1849 the weather was typically changeable. The 19th was a bright cold morning with the wind in the north. He writes:- 'Observed the ducks playing in the water, dashing about and diving. We shall find what this presages. It perhaps does not refer to the weather but to some other cause and feeding.'

The next day it was still bright but frosty and very cold.
'If the ducks can foresee change in weather they are long-sighted as there is no change as yet.'

On 21st the wind was 'direct south, very mild morning. The ducks are perhaps right yet, but we shall see.'

The weather improvement continued and on 25th, 'Wind in the south - fine vernal day. The ducks seem to have prognosticated well.'

Returning from Wythburn on the Sunday of this week Parson Lawson saw an eagle, unusual as by then the eagle had ceased to breed in the Lake District. During the eighteenth century sheep farmers regarded the eagle as a pest and according to Pearson and Pennington in the Lake District, New Naturalist Series, 1973, farmers at Rosthwaite destroyed the eggs and eyries of the eagles that tried to nest in Borrowdale, reckoning that each eyrie cost one lamb a day. The parish paid one shilling for each eagle destroyed.

The 'Dotterell on Helvellyn' tales of which had aroused the parson's interest earlier, was also rare, nesting only occasionally on rocky ground over 2500 ft. Eudromias Morinellus is a member of the plover family which winters in North Africa flying back to nest sometimes in northern England but nowadays mainly in the Cairngorms. In former times it was eaten as a delicacy so gourmets and egg collectors drastically reduced its numbers.

The last day of April 1849 and at last the affirmation of the coming of the spring. 'Cuckoo heard by J. Westray and later perhaps the same day 'Heard the cuckoo and saw swallows', then for the third time Parson Lawson notes. 'The cuckoo has been heard on the 7th of this month.' He mentioned this on 27th April and had already written down the information from Mrs. Westray that she had heard its call on the 7th April 1840. It is unlikely that she wrote to The Times but the note of the cuckoo, heard after a long dark winter was, and still is, a reason for rejoicing and is part of the folk-lore of Cumbria. Maybe today's lakeland dwellers do not often quote the old proverb that Parson Lawson wrote in his first Cumbrian entry 'When cuckoo comes to ye thorn that's bare you may sell the Cow, the corn to spare.' but a friend who has lived all her life in Matterdale vouches for the fact that the call of the cuckoo is still eagerly awaited and news of its arrival passed on. Farming people, she says, will nod their heads over a sickly beast and say 'It'll not hear cuckoo again.'
It is said that in times past dwellers in Borrowdale were so convinced that the cuckoo was responsible for longer days and warmer weather, that they tried to build a fence to keep the bird in the valley. The dalesmen were henceforth known as 'Borrowdale Gowks'. A 'gowk' being the local term for cuckoo.

The transient cuckoo seems almost mystical. It certainly exercised the thoughts of the Wythburn curate.

'29th May 1849 Cuckoo falters in his note.

4th June . . Cuckoo hoarse.'

Next year 1850 he first heard the cuckoo and saw swallows on 3rd May but wrote that 'Ritson of St. John's saw a flock of swallows a fortnight before.' On the 21st June 'cuckoo still strong in note', but by 27th 'Cuckoo gone not heard since Monday 24th.'

In 1851 Parson Lawson first heard the cuckoo on Sunday 20th April and last on 30th June, noting on July 1st 'Cuckoo gone.' but on 21st July adds 'saw a cuckoo in the Park when in company with Messrs. H. and Dodson - no mistake'

Two farmers Reuben Thwaite of Dalehead farm and William Wilson of Armboth were so pleased to hear the bird that they passed the news around. On April 23rd 1852 the parson notes down the information from them. Two days later confirming springtime he 'saw a swallow as coming from Chapel' and then by 24th June, 'Cuckoo gone, 1st heard on Sunday 20th'.

Observation is always keen and pleasure in wildlife clear. In February 1850 thrushes were singing and birds whistling and a bat was seen for the first time, even earlier than that he and his wife watched in March the previous year. On March 1st 1850 'wagtail arrived and yellow hammer'. At the end of April 'The wild fowl which wintered on Thirlmere left it about the beginning of this month. Two large ducks called shell ducks remain and appear to have made their nest on a small island.' Marking the end of summer in 1851 'Swallows not gone' on 14th October but on the 18th 'Swallows gone'.

Fishing was obviously a favourite spring time occupation for the parson and he enjoyed the sport alone and in company. Within weeks of his arrival he was contemplating the possibilities.

'1849 April 5th very few flies on the water as yet.

April 11th nothing to be done in fishing - bad season.

April 26th Heavy showers early in the morning a bright day with wind south - very seasonable very like a fishing day.

May 18th Westray caught a pike 9lb.

May 21st Fished for the first time. Fish would not rise expecting more rain, and being glutted already.

May 24th Fished St. John's beck - no sport.

May 31st Cloudy day - evening like rain. Trout wont show themselves at the bridge.

September 10th Wind S. cloudy morning, showery good fishing

September 27th Fish wd not rise.' And so that season ended. 1850 began badly.

'April 1st I fished for ye first time - nil

April 3rd fished for ye 2nd time - Nil

May 12th Fished St. John's with Dodson fair sport

May 27th Fished Wythburn heads - fair sport

May 29th Fished red tarn - nil

Aug 6th Fished Wythburn no b.'

All told fair for the year, 1851 began better.

'April 21st Fished St. John's 1st time this season killed one, Mr. Hardisty - one'

Fortune lapsed again.

'May 9th fished Wythburn with Mr. Hardisty - O

May 28th fished ye lake with Messrs Pratt & Hardisty O'

Then in June '7th fished Wythburn . . 15. with Mr. Dodson

13th fished Wythburn . . 5.' If these are the number of fish caught they were indeed rising for the parson.

On May 12th 1852 'Fished for the 1st time at Legber caught two'

Style End (Steel End now West Head Farm) Wythburn.

Sketch of ruined cottage. Site unknown.

The phrases are brief but can stir the imagination of any fisherman strolling by the becks and lake almost one hundred and forty years later.

Fishing began with the cuckoo call in April; fox hunting began in September. On 24th of that month 1849 'Crosher hunted for the first time this season.' Previously in August Parson Lawson had noted that two puppies had arrived from Croshers for someone called Rauthwell. In June the same name is mentioned 'H. Rauthwell and Lester came.'

Crosher must be John Crozier of Threlkeld and so renowned were his dogs that the puppies would be sold far afield.

Under the title of 'A North Country Nimrod.', Canon H. D. Rawnsley devotes a chapter of his Lake Country Sketches to a colourful account of life of John Crozier. When he died in 1903 at the Riddings in the shadow of Blencathra, Crozier was the oldest Master of the Hunt in Britain and had been Master of the Blencathra pack for over sixty years, half of them at his own expense. His father turned over the mastership of the Threlkeld dogs to his son in 1840 when John was eighteen years old. The pack then numbered about six couples. They were kept on farms around all the year and trained to meet at the sound of the Master's horn. The Blencathra pack is now kennelled at Threlkeld but out of season still sent out and kept by local farmers. This is known as 'walking the dogs'.

It is believed that John Crozier improved the breed of his hounds by getting a strain from John Peel's kennels. When Parson Lawson came to Wythburn John Peel was in his seventies and still hunting. The young Master Crozier but twenty seven already had a reputation as a kind hearted and generous man, best friend of dogs and worst enemy of foxes.

Evidently the parson took a great interest in the hunt which was part of the life of the dalesfolk. The packs of hounds developed from the few hounds kept by farmers to control predatory foxes. Gradually the farmers began to organise hunts, particularly in spring to protect the lambing flocks. The church was also involved. Victoria County History for Cumbria mentions that Ancient Books of Churchwarden's accounts contain numberless entries of payments made for heads of foxes, a guinea for a greyhound fox, 10s a cub. V.C.H. also tells about how the information about forthcoming hunt fixtures was made public. Immediately after the service the parish clerk wound mount a tombstone in the churchyard and announce to the assembled crowd the dates and plans for meets and auctions.

Parson Lawson may or may not have done this at Wythburn but he certainly had news of the hunts.

'February 4th 1850 Crosher at Gate Crag & Bields. March 20th Crosher's hounds killed a fox in Grasmere.'

To have given such a long run this was most likely one of the greyhound foxes of the churchwarden's accounts. Longer in the leg and heavier than the present day foxes, they frequented the high ground making earths in rocks and cairns or in cracks in rock faces. These foxes are rare today, if not extinct, in the Lake District. The reddish brown shorter legged fox hunted by present fell packs has different habits and is more likely to be found around the timber producing woodlands no longer patrolled by gamekeepers.

Also in March 1850 Parson Lawson wrote 'Heads hounds killed a Martin or Mart.' The Pine-Martin, Sweet Mart or Crag Mart made its home amongst the crags, descending to raid rabbit warrens and according to V.C.H. 1901 was a game and resourceful quarry, hunted by venerable sportsmen in many a spirited chase.

The implication being that it was by then, scarce. Pine Martens are still rare but believed to have returned and to be breeding in the Grisedale Forest.

That hunting was necessary is born out in a report in the Cumberland Pacquet of January 22nd 1850.

'The neighbourhood of Hutton Hall the seat of Sir Henry Vane, literally swarms with foxes which almost nightly commit depredations in the adjacent farm yards, some farmers having had nearly the whole of their poultry destroyed by these nocturnal marauders. At the close of the present frost it is confidently expected that the young Baronet will invite Mr. Crozier and Mr. Peel to try their well known packs in the locality of the hall.'

Parson Lawson makes notes of fox hunts each season with Meets at Legberthwaite, Armboth, Wythburn and Trespath, (The old name for Thirlspot.) On September 1st 1852 he enjoyed 'Fine hunting with Sir H. Vane's hounds.' The Squire of Hutton Hall, then aged twenty-three and Lord of the Manor of Wythburn loved his sport and some twenty-five years later only agreed to sell his land to Manchester Waterworks Committee on condition that he kept the rights of shooting and sporting over Armboth fells for the rest of his life.

Another pack mentioned as hunting in Wythburn during a week of lovely weather in February 1851 is Geldert's Hounds. Like John Crozier, Mr. Gelderd of Nell House, now the Patterdale Hotel maintained the pack at his own expense. His Patterdale Pack was amalgamated with the Bald How (Matterdale) hounds to form the Ullswater Foxhounds.

Taking pleasure in a popular and essential part of the sporting life of his parish at that time, Parson Lawson on March 9th 1852 was 'out on Helvellyn with Crosher's dogs' and two days later again 'killed a fox.'

FARMING MATTERS

It is not surprising that Parson Lawson's first remarks concerning farming mention the lambing season. Sheep on the fells are a cherished part of the Lakeland scene and they have grazed the slopes since Neolithic settlers brought in their domestic animals. The Romans may have added some strains but the hardy Herdwicks are generally supposed to have been introduced by the Norsemen. In the Medieval period vast flocks of sheep, tended by the monks from the great monastic houses of Furness, Fountains, Holme Cultram and Shap altered the vegetational pattern and shaped the landscape. Demand for wool grew. Armies through the ages have had to be clothed and until 1814 everyone not only wore but was buried shrouded in woollen cloth. Industrialisation and Victorian prosperity created a demand for upholstery and carpets for which the coarse fleeces of the fell sheep were eminently suitable.

When his car is halted on the wide road slashing through from Thirlspot to Shoulthwaite, today's visitor may sit patiently and watch the bobbing heads of the gathered flocks or in his holiday cottage nearby, he may endure tolerantly the incessant baa-ing of a hundred male lambs awaiting transport to the lowland fattening fields because he feels that this activity has an aura of permanence in a changing world. Hopefully, he is right but he and his kind plus subsidies, the National Trust and the authorities of the National Park are all now necessary to keep the rhythm of the sheep-farming year as an integral part of the life of the district.

However in the mid nineteenth century the farmers in the Vale of Thirlmere would obtain anything above a subsistence standard of living from the sale of sheep or their meat and wool. There would be some income from resident miners and tourists and any other surplus produce could be sold at market in Keswick or Penrith.

There is no better way to give a picture of farming in the valley before the Manchester Waterworks Scheme began than to extract the entries concerned with farming from the diary and reassemble them in sequence.

Extracts from Rev. Basil R. Lawson's diary which deal with farming practices in the Vale of Thirlmere 1849-1852.

1849
Apr. 27 Lambs were playing this afternoon.
Apr. 28 Lambing season very favourable so far.
May 3 field carrots sewn.
June 20 washed the sheep.
June 22 sowed guano on the onions.
July 10 Dalehead clipping.
July 11 sheep clipped.
July 21 carried Hodgin Hill.

1850
March 4 Reuben breaking up the meadows in front of the Kings Head.
April 4 J. Westray breaking up the great field.
June 18 Geo. Wilson's sheep washing
June 19 Everything looks promising for farmers.
June 20 Dalehead sheep washing.
July 8 Geo. Wilson's clipping.
July 9 Dalehead clipping.
July 11 J. Weightman's clipping.
Aug. 7 fine - finished the hay.
Sep. 6 J. Westray began to reap his oats.
Nov. 2 tup fair at Keswick.
1851
Feb. 24-25 Last two days cutting timber.
April 24 potatoes planted.
May 7 warm-growing weather.
June 26 D. Thwaite washed the sheep.
July 8 n.w. wet-wet was to have been the Dalehead clipping.
July 16 Geo. Wilson's clipping.
Aug. 30 J.W. began to reap.
Sep. 16 J. Westray finished reaping.
Sep. 20 finished harvest.

1852
March 16 J. W. sowed the oats.
March 19 planted the field potatoes.
March 23 finished field potatoes.
March 30 D. Thwaite sowing oats in the front field.
April 27 J. W. cutting peats.
June 22 John Gillbanks washed sheep.
June 23 D. Thwaite washed his sheep.

June 30 - a fine vegetating month.
July 6 J. W. began to mow.
July 12 Geo. Wilson's clipping.
July 13 Dalehead clipping.
July 15 T. Weightman's clipping.
July 21 v.fine carried hay.
July 24 first rate hay weather.
Aug. 16 J.W. began to reap.
Aug. 20 J. Westray carried his grain and finished.
Oct. 13 sow littered 18 pigs.

Sheep clipping was in one sense a harvest time for the sheep farmer. After the animals had been gathered, washed and rested each farm had its recognised clipping day in July and the families and farm hands took turns to help each other. All would work together. While skilled men did the clipping, younger boys would bring the sheep to them and tie the kicking legs. Still younger children stood by with 'sauve', a mixture of tar and grease to dab on an accidental nick. Girls and women busied themselves preparing food and bringing drinks to the men. At night when all was done, there would be shepherds' songs, maybe a fiddler would play for dancing. Hard work indeed but with it came the pleasure of a shared activity, a good deal of 'crack' (gossip) and the knowledge that all would benefit in turn which was the bedrock of life in the small community. That Parson Lawson enjoyed and was part of it all was known far and wide. The writer of his obituary in the Westmorland Gazette remembered and recorded the fact.

The routine of 'breaking-up', hay-making, reaping and harvest provided for humans, horses, cattle, pigs and sheep. Carrots, onions and potatoes are grown for household use and stock. 'Guano' on the onions, is the local term for anything except farmyard manure but there were at Kendal, 'Importers of Guano' listed in the 1829 P & W.* Timber would have many uses including fuel and John Westray also 'cuts peat' on April 27 1852. Peat is formed on many of the plateau areas where surface water excludes oxygen and deposition of vegetable matter occurs slowly. Its existence made possible the siting of isolated farm dwellings, was used by the 16th century German miners and dug on the uplands between Thirlmere and Borrowdale and also around Threlkeld. Peat, for fuel is usually cut in the summer, when it is least moist and then stacked to dry out further. Cutting so early was probably unusual to cause the parson to mention it but by April 27th that year he had recorded seven or eight weeks of continuous cold but dry weather.

The last entry for any of the three years again concerns the sheep. Nov.2nd. 'Tup fair at Keswick.'

Tups are the rams bought or hired to be put to the ewes by the end of November and ensure that the lambs would be there again in the spring.

There are still plenty of sheep on the remaining fields adjacent to the Kings Head and at the northern end of Thirlmere. On improved leys grass is cut green these days, there are no carrots, onions, potatoes or oats to be seen. There are car parks, caravans and tents. The days of the interdependent community working together and wasting nothing are but a memory.

* Parson and White Directory.

Great Howe, Legberthwaite.

High Stennack, Wythburn.
Home of 'Old Nancy' Dowson. Demolished.

THE FARMERS OF WYTHBURN. 1851 Census

Hollin Brow	Ferdinand Cole	30 acres
Horse Head	Jane Hawkrigg	
Low Horse Head	Martha Olifer	12 acres
Steel End	Joshua Dover	54 acres
Stenkin	Thomas Wilson	27 acres
Waisthead (Westhead)	John Gillbanks	51 acres
Stennack	John Dawson	25 acres
City	John Birkett	58 acres
Bank	James Hind	45 acres
Armboth	Geroge Wilson	70 acres
Armboth House	Jane Westray	30 acres
Nether Place	Thomas Weightman	40 acres
Smethwaite	Isaac Carmel	40 acres
Bridge End	Isaac Bristo	67 acres
Green	John Dowthwaite	14 acres
Stanah	John Hawkrigg	30 acres
Stybeck	Charles Birkett (blacksmith)	11 acres
Fisher Place	Joseph Wilkinson	70 acres
Threlspot	John Atkinson (Kings Head)	30 acres
Dalehead	Daniel Thwaite	150 acres

(Spelling as enumerator) Each farm had certain stints or areas for grazing on the fells. Stocks kept up to strength would keep to their own boundaries. There are no walls or fences on higher Pastures.

AT CHAPEL.

Mention 'Wytheburn's modest House of prayer' and most people will add the next phrase 'As lowly as the lowliest dwelling.' Few will continue with the succeeding lines from 'The Waggoner' by William Wordsworth, which tell that the building lacked a clock but had two little bells in the belfry. Hartley Coleridge, however was sure that the humble chapel had a single bell. Canon H. D. Rawnsley, by 1894 wished that the good fairies would take away in the night the well dressed stones of the new belfry which had been built by the Manchester Authorities along with other works, including the strengthening of the old bridge at Armboth, to soften opposition to their Waterworks Scheme. The Canon wondered for how many years the little bell had hung in its simple cobblestone rough cast belfry. Certainly before and when Parson Lawson first preached at Wythburn in February 1849.

There are stories, repeated with varying details in many books about Lakeland, concerning other parsons and their flock at Wythburn. One curate was said to have dropped his sermon notes down a crack between the pulpit and the wall. The congregation thought they they were going to get away without a homily on that day, but he read a long chapter from the Bible instead, saying that it was worth ten of his sermons anyway.

Another anecdote is of the bell-ringer who was found sitting astride the roof ridge ringing the bell by hand. Some versions say that the rope had been eaten by sheep, others that Jemmy Hawkrigg had taken it to pull his hay cart.

Smalthwaite
&
Smeathwaite bridge
St John's. Cumberland

Glencoin. VIEW from Helluellyn. Ullswater. splendedior vitro Crossfell, in the distance.

These legendary tales can be taken further with a family story from Miss Ada Ranaldson Hallam, granddaughter of the Rev. Basil Lawson.

'One hot summer day, a little lamb ran in at the open door, looked up at my grandfather preaching, said Baa very loudly, and ran out again.'

This tale re-told to a child born after her grandfather was laid to rest in his churchyard surely shows the affection which he aroused in family and parishioners. There are other homely touches revealed in the brief facts that Parson Lawson records about chapel life.

'Aug 4 1850 Little Westray christened'

'Nov 16 ½ yrs salary due

Nov 17 average cong. half years salary due

Nov 23 went to Keswick RECEIVED SALARY.'

'Nov 17 1851 Stove came to Wythburn. Nov 21st put up stove.'

In the stone built chapel with a stone flagged floor the stove must have been very welcome.

On 24th February 24th 1850 Parson Lawson writes 'My wife at Wythburn.' Earlier he had entered Jan 16th 'my little girl born at Legberthwaite'. Four days later the baby died, so this was probably the first time that his wife was at chapel after this sadness. In 1852 on March 14th he took the four year old Basil with him and wrote, it seems with pride

'BAZZY at CHAPEL for the first time.'

Another happy family occasion was the 19th September 1852 when daughter Ellen was christened. He had his little girl.

For the years 1849 and 1850 the actual numbers of persons attending chapel are only occasionally recorded, 56 in June 1850, 16 communicants on July 21st. He notes on July 28th 'an average congregation 20 full grown persons.' and on Xmas Day 1850 11 communicants.

In 1851 a Religious Census was taken in Britain. Maybe this prompted Parson Lawson as it is then he starts recording in his diary some attendance figures for Wythburn. Previously he had described the congregation with the terms 'good, moderate, average, small, thin, tolerable.'

In 1851 and 1852 the congregation does not again reach the 56 of June 9th 1850, but the numbers may refer only to the communicants and range from 4 to 48.

The 1851 general census put the population of Wythburn at 203 persons. The Religious census for that year (published by Horace Mann in 1854) says that although the statistics were collected on a very wet day throughout Britain, attendance at churches and chapels was assessed at 51% overall. For Cumberland and Westmorland it was 25 - 33% of population. Parson Lawson's attendances were probably near to the low point of that figure.

Sometimes when the weather was at its worst there was no one there when he got to chapel and there were times when wind and floods prevented him from going. Only once does he mention after being at chapel on the Sunday 30th May 1852 that the next day he was very ill. Also there is only one occasion when he records that anyone else took a service for him. May 17th 1849 'Mr. Bush preached for me.' This was Paul Bush, curate at St. John's in the Vale.

Twice Rev. Lawson mentions Confirmation days at Keswick when he would accompany to Crosthwaite the candidates, to whom he had taught their catechism, to be blessed by Bishop Percy. The Bishop would also be present to assess the work of his clergy at the Visitation at Penrith on June 27th 1850 and at

Wigton on June 9th 1852. Parson Lawson does not say that he was there himself but was bound to be interested in the news of these diocesan inspections.

The 'Cumberland Pacquet' of Tuesday July 16th 1850 carries the following report:-

> 'A numerous meeting of clergymen was held at the Royal Oak in Keswick on Thursday last in support of the Carlisle Diocesan Society for Promoting Christian Knowledge and the Society for the Relief of Widows and Orphans of Necessitous Clergymen and the Carlisle Diocesan Clergy Aid Society. Rt. Rev. Dr. Percy, Lord Bishop of Carlisle presided.'

Was Parson Lawson there or was he at Weightman's clipping at Nether Place, Armboth, which also took place on that day? It is a fair guess which event he would prefer. Perhaps he managed both.

On March 23rd 1851 a note of 'A subs - for the Soc-prop Gosp 1/1 one shilling and one penny!!!' leaves one wondering whether the Parson considered the 'mod: congregation' to be ungenerous. He must have encouraged them for in 1852 on June 24th a 'Collection for churches' yielded '12/4 at Chapel' and on July 3rd the augmented sum 15/- was remitted for 'Soc'y for Churches' (at Keswick).

Other entries in the little book show a patient ministry to his people from christening to the last rites. Through the years the work became more and the chapelry became a parish in 1867. Eventually Parson Lawson cared for the thousands of workmen and their families, housed in temporary huts at Wythburn, Armboth and Legberthwaite or lodging in the farm houses.

Miss Ada Hallam writes of the impressions passed on to her:- 'Manchester murdered Wythburn and Mardale. My grandfather hated it of course, but got on well with the navvies. After his death, his successor (Mr. Hill) gave out one Sunday that it was proposed to put in a memorial window to the Rev. B. Lawson, and that during the week Mrs. Easton (Nags Head) and Miss Dawson (Schoolmistress) would go round the village collecting - And a navvy who was sitting at the bottom of the church, stood up, and said "I beg to second that motion".'

The Rev. Winfried Des Voex Hill was the second Vicar of Wythburn and ministered for thirty-two years, seeing most of the remaining homes evacuated and demolished, the dam opened, the valley flooded and the new road built along the western shore of the reservoir. He lived in the Vicarage, built for and first occupied by the Rev. Lawson and his family in 1862. The stone building, remembered by local people as in a lovely garden and covered with climbing roses was demolished after the Union of the Benefices in 1926 when Wythburn became part of the parish of St. John's in the Vale. Rev. C. G. Darrell the present Vicar describes the church as 'like a stranded boat without an ocean to sail on or a crew.'

It is, however still loved and kept immaculate. The Vicar, his parishioners, other Cumbrians and tourists worship there on certain Sundays in the year. Many visitors for many reasons come from far and near and look around and inside the low white isolated chapel. Some come for prayer and quietness or to be thankful for the beauty of the scenes around them. Some are interested in the fabric, the history or the literary associations of Wythburn. Some are just curious or want to get out of the rain. All will leave enriched.

Note March 16 – the day that we arrived at Legberthwaite was unusually mild. In the eveng. Mrs L— and I watched a bat for some time, a sight uncommon at this season of the year. We have not seen it again and this day is the 5th of April. Have noticed the yellow wagtail, (Motacilla flava of Ray) this last week this day being the 7th of April. April 16 – Mr Westmorland arrived.

Sand Snipes on ye banks of Thirlmere. Dottrel on Helvellyn. The cuckoo was heard by Mrs Westray on the 7th of April – 1840 in Legberthwaite.

In the year 1749, Augst 22, – A thunderstorm washed away the mill at Legberthwaite – the mill stones were never again found. In 1811, May 11th a thunder storm broke over Threlkeld on ye Sunday mornig which washed away a house & flooded ye valley. In 1846 an awful tempest raged over Legberthwaite & Legberthwaite which did much injury.

Notes of Weather – beginning April 1st 1849.

April 1st	S.	Wind S. E. Fair, but cold. Eveng. Thunder with hail.	
2nd		Ditto.	
3rd		Wind S. E. mild & spring like. Evening, thunder with hail.	
4th		Wind in the same quarter. Sunny but chill. Thunder at a distance, little rain.	
5th		Mornig. Wet with an East wind. Eveng. clear and mild. Very few flies on the water as yet.	
6th		Good Friday. Wind S. E. Fine spring weather. cold at night.	party on Helvellyn. Kendal Bumps.
7th		Dark lowering mornig, & cold.	
8th	S	Easter day. Wind northerly. Dark & showering day. very little improvement in vegetation. Eveng, fair. Moon in her 3rd qr.	For the next fortnight we shall find ye wind to prevail northerly.
9th		Wet and cold.	
10th		Wind north. very cold but fine. Two tourists attempted to ascend Helvellyn – obliged to give it up, wind so high – could not stand.	
11th		Dark & cloudy mornig. Wind northy. nothing to be done in fishing – bad season. Sleet showers. ~~Heavy~~	
12th		Bright but cold. Heavy rain at night. Wind N. west. In ye Eveng – W, southerly.	
13th		Wind west – fells covered with snow. Sunny & warm.	
14th		Snow showers – Wind, N. The month so far with short intervals, has been inclement.	
15th	S	Snow on ye hills, cold N, E. wind.	
16th		Morning mild & sunny – afterwards showery, but mild & growing. Wind westerly.	
17th		Hard frost overnight. Bright & Sunny, with snow showers – very cold. W.N, E. No prospect of fine weather.	

18th Frost at nightfall. Fine & Sunny - milder than it was before. In the evening the wind veered to the South, accompanied with snow & rain.

19th Morning bright but cold - Wind due north. Observed the ducks playing in the water, dashing about & diving. We shall find what this presages. It perhaps does not refer to the weather but to some other cause & feeling. Snow in Leicestershire (Mailstone) 4 inch deep.

20th Bright morning. Frost in the night. very cold. If the ducks can bode a change in weather, they are long sighted as there is no change as yet.
Evening - clouds lower than the Armboth Fells, slowly creeping along. Wind on the Horn, - mild as Midsummer - tho' there was a thin cloud of snow enveloping, passing away to the South. Mr Bird called.

This state of the cloud appears to be a favorable symptom so far and it is now the 25th

21st Wind, direct South & very mild morning. The ducks are perhaps right yet, but we shall see. Horse worse this morning. Evening - calm. W, N, again

22nd S Wind, direct South. Snow storm & sleet. very cold. Cleared up towards evening. Saw an eagle on returning from Wythburn.

Horse died.

23rd Morning W. Sud. turning mild. fine Sunny afternoon. Evening, W. North.

24th Morning fine & bright. Wind, South. Cloudy in the afternoon. Night W, S. ~~dark & rainy temperature cold.~~

25th Wind in the South - fine vernal day. walked to Threlkeld between dinner and tea - grasses more forwarder there than at Legberthwaite.
The ducks seem to have prognosticated well.

Heard from Revd R. W. Whitby.

26th Heavy Shower early in the morning, a bright day with wind, South. very

27th W. S. Showery morning - clouds dense offered a bright sunny day succeeded. Wind very high & cold. Lambs were playing this afternoon, sign of rain and it has arrived in earnest.
When the wind drops we shall probably have warmth. No swallows as yet. On the seventh of April 1840 the cuckoo was heard in Legberthwaite.
Rain ceased before bed time.

The Belfast almanack has been correct in its prognostications for the month.

28th Morning fine & springlike. A beautiful day. Evening, wind in the West, - calm & settled to all appearance. Silky clouds hang over Saddleback. Lambing season very favorable so far.

Heard of the Revd Hastwell

29th S. Fine spring weather, - tho occasionally threatening rain.

Cuckoo and Swallows seen in Wythburn

30th Lovely morning - Cuckoo heard by J Westray. Ascended Helvellyn - found it warm with a gentle breeze - the Sun created a murky atmosphere, so that I could not enjoy any distant view. I fancy that no one had been there before me this year. humbug, I said.
A party was up on Good friday - snobs of course.

Cavalts sown Spenall etc. Heard of Cuckoo and saw swallows. The cuckoo has been heard on the 7th of this one

May. May.

1st Commences with a lovely summer morning. as ———

2 W. North. Fine & mild, but cloudy. Gent. from Lincolnshire arrived at night, lost on Whiteside. Went with him into Borradale & thence to Keswick & returned to dinner.
Evening - W, North

3rd W, N. beautiful weather.

Field Carrots sown

4th W, S, E. a good breeze but warm. 9 p.m. wind South - beautiful moon light & mild.

very cold, & blows like rain, but no appearance of it. Sky clear. | [illegible]

6th S Morning fine S.W., N, E. In the Evening very cold. Wind high. Heard of Miss Skelton — | Bragg preached at St Johns.

7th W. N. fine

8th W. E. bright but cold. | Heard from the Revd Whitley T. O.

9th W. N. cloudy. Tourists increase, spavined, wind galled & sore footed.

10th Little or no wind — very mild, but cloudy. Rather inclined to rain.

11th W. N. cloudy & betokening rain. | The cold weather has stopped the flight of tourists.

12th W. S. W. Cloudy with occasional gleams of sunshine — No rain as yet. | Have not seen any for two days. They are a [illegible] bird; not found in White nor mentioned by Ray.

13th S Morning wet with wind S. West. fine growing day.

14th A showery morning W. S. West. Cleared up towards Noon. A very favourable day for vegetation. | [illegible] have noticed ye shake in ye [illegible] of ye [illegible]

15th W. S. W. Morning fair — but cloudy. little rain fallen in ye night. planted one little potatoe which I found in ye road. | Tourists have vanished. Those who came [illegible] carried a [illegible] [illegible] back with the [illegible] Edwards was to be married.

16th Wind S. West — mild rain

17th Similar to ye preceding. (Ascension day) Keswick fair day. | Mr Bush preached for me.

18th W. S. W. Morning cloudy & betokening rain. Evening — W. N. West. wet night | Westray caught a Pike — 9lb.

19th W. N. very fine and [illegible] [illegible]

20 S W. S. Heavy [illegible] [illegible] [illegible] | Heard from Sir Wolstan.

21st W. S. Fine [illegible]. [illegible] [illegible] [illegible] & night. | Fished for ye 1st time. Fish

---

[illegible] rain [illegible] being [illegible] [illegible] [illegible]

22nd W. S. very wet morning — ye rest fine. Evening threatened rain.

23rd W. S. very wet.

24th W. S. day cloudy & overcast, wind strong. Jane Whitley married. | Fished St Johns beck — no sport. Took my wife and Bazzy to ye top of Great Howe.

25th Morning — W. N. got round to ye South before 11 a.m. Sunny day. | Received wedding cards from Mr & Mrs Wilkin —

26th (Friday) At 12 at night stars shone brightly from my sleeping room window, at 3, stars were gone and the sky cloudy. It has rained since 5 — W. S. very wet. | Whit Saturday

27 S. W. S. very warm & sunny. | Whitsunday.

28 W. S. do in other respects. | Mrs L. and Bazzy went to ye water fall at Fisher place.

29th W. S. W. fine and bright — Evening like for rain. | Cuckoo falters in his note.

30 W. N. W. fine. Walked on the fell — a party from Carlisle, 120 in number arrived. | Shock of an Earth quake.

31st W. S. W. cloudy day. Evening like rain, trout were shew themselves at the bridge. | Took my wife round by Raven Crag. famous pedestrian

June.

1st W. S. W. Rain during the preceding night, but fine Summer weather.

2nd S W. S. W. very warm, but showery in ye morning.

3rd S W. S. W. Summer weather. | Heard from Mr Hooke.

4th W. S. W. very sultry. thunder in ye air. | Cuckoo — hoarse.

5th S. W. very warm | went [illegible]

6th Do | [illegible]

7th Excessively hot. | walked to Keswick

8th W. S. W in ye morning — Evening East. came on very hazy. | climbed Helvellyn with [illegible] and Lloyd.

9th W. S. W. very hot.

10th S. W. N. E. Snow on the fells, down to the [illegible]. | Knubley called.

11th W. N. Fine & bright day. Evening cloudy and cold. — the bracken clock very plentiful this year. Unknown warm weather

12th W. N. Dark morning - bright day, with cold breeze.

13th W. N. bright with thunder spots.

14th W. N. W. warm and sunny. Took my wife on Skiddaw, started at 12 p.m., returned at 6 p.m. — a fine view of the Solway firth and Morecambe bay.

15th W. S. W. - Sultry.

16th W. westerly, very bold close. Hail shower in the afternoon. — Confirmation day at Keswick.

17th S W. N. W. bright but cold.

18th W. S. W. cloudy but mild.

19th W. W. wet morning - fine rain & warm

20th W. S. W. bright summer day. — washed the sheep

21st W. N. W. bright but cold.

22nd S. W. cloudy morning & day. Evening rain. — several swans on the Drains.

23rd W. S. W. cloudy morning, - bright evening.

24th S W. S. W. by W. bright & sunny.

25th W. N. W. dark and sultry. — H. Rawthwaite & Lesher Crane

26th W. S. W. bright and warm.

27th W. N. W. dark & cold.

28th W. W. [illegible] weather.

29th W. W. cloudy. Slight shower. Evening, wet. — cloudbursts on along the side of Aran both fell.

30th W. N. E. fine but cold.

July

1st S Morning W. S. W. & misty. afternoon heavy rain, & W. South. Evening very wet, and W. [illegible].

2nd W. N. W. Showery morning.

3rd W. S. W. very wet day.

4th W. S. W. Showery. Evening wet.

5th W. S. W. Fine summer weather.

6th W. S. W. Very wet day.

7th W. still S. W. and continual rain.

8th S W. W. fair & sunny.

9th W. S. W. bright morning, warm throughout the day.

10th W. N. W. very warm & dry. — Birkhead clipping

11th W. N. W. the same — sheep clipped.

12th W. S. W. very hot.

13th W. S. W. sultry, but cloudy.

14th No alteration - very hot.

15th S [illegible]

16th

17th W. [illegible] in the day - fine afterwards. — Mr Bragg breakfasted with us.

18th W. S. [illegible]

19th W. S. [illegible]

20th W. N. fine.

21st W. N. dark & [illegible]

22nd S W. S. dark [illegible]

23rd W. S. W. dark & wet — Miss Lawson arrived

24th W. S. W. dark and showery [illegible] the north [illegible] wet

25th wind changed again to the S. bright W. N. W. & wet.

26th W. N. W. fair.

27th W. N. fine [illegible] — Miss L. left us.

28th W. S. W. very wet Evening.

29th S W. S. fine.

30th W. W. Showery. Evening thunder.

31st W. N. W. Fine; thunder at a distance.

August.

1st W. N. W. fine. [illegible] & ragged.

2. W. N. W. a calm [illegible] dull morning. afternoon & evening [illegible] from the north with drizzling rain. [illegible] night in the north. — 2 puppies arrived from Crookers for Rawlinson

3rd W. N. fine.

4th W. N. Sunny in the [illegible] cloudy evening.

5th S W. N. Fine but cloudy. — Heard from Bill Baker.

6th W. E. fine & sultry. — puppies well.

7th W. S. W. wet afternoon.

8th W. S. cloudy. Showers.

9th W. S. W. Morning fine - Evening wet.

10th W. if any, south. Evening very misty.

11th W. S. W. [illegible]

12 S W. S. cloudy & showers. Evening fine.

13. W. S. Very wet.

14 W. S. W. wet

15 W. S. W. showery.

16 W. S. W. showery.

17 W. N. W. fine afternoon & Evening.

18 W. N. W. Showery.

19 S W. W. fine but cloudy.

20 W. S. W. fine but dark. — coach broke down

21 W. S. W. Misty morning - afternoon fine. Crossed Hodgin hill. — visited St John's Beck with Mr. J. Mann

22 [illegible]
23. W.S.W. fine - Eveng W.N. fine - — Mr. Mason left.
24 W.S. fine. Eveng - W.N. fine.
25. W.W. dark & drizzling
26 S W.S.W. wet - afternoon W.W. fine
27 W.N.W. dark morng.
28. W.S.W. cloudy morng - afternoon misty.
29 W.N. Misty morng.
30 W.N. very wet. — — Keswick sports
31. W.W. fair, dark day. Eveng very fine

Septembr.

1 W.S.W. dark & sultry.
2nd S W.S.W. thunder lightg very wet. afternoon fine & showery
3rd W.S. very warm
4 W.S. hot morng. afternoon W.N.E. hot.
5 W.N.E. very sultry.
6 W.N.E. morng hot - Noon misty - Eveng cool. — Lord Langdale on Helvellyn
7 W.N.E. very hot & showery.
8 W.S. very fine & warm.
9 S W.S. cloudy morng - showery.
10 W.S. morng showery - fine & sunny. — good fishing
11 W.W. morng misty - afternoon wet. — went to Lazonby Dede 24 June 1840.
12 W.W. fine.
13 W.N.W. fine.
14 W.N.W. fine
15 W.N.W. fine.
16 S W.N.W. morng wet; afternoon fine. — — at Ainstable
17 W.N.W. fine.
18 W.N.W. fine. — — — returned from Lazonby.
19 W.N.W. fine.
20 W.N. morng cloudy - fells misty;
21 W.N.E. slight showers and dark day.
22 W.N.E. fair but cloudy.
23 S W.N.E. fine & sunny. — Crosher hunted for the first time this season.
24 — W.E. fine & sunny —
25 — W.E. fine.
26 — W.N.E. fine - Eveng W.S.E.
27 — W.S.E. fine - Eveng W.N.E. — fish wd not rise.
28 — W.N.E. wet - Eveng fine.
29 W.S.E. misty & damp.
30 S W.N.E. very wet. - Eveng fair.

October.

1 .. W.N.E. fine but cloudy - Eveng showery

2 .. W N.W. [illegible] — [illegible] snow [illegible]
3 .. W N.W. cloudy fine afternoon snow
4 .. W N.E. snowing on Helvellyn - fine but cold — for
5 .. W N.E. [illegible] cold — — Mr. Dodson arrived.
6 .. W N.W. hard frost. Eveng fine
7 S. .. W N.W. hard frost.
8 .. W N.W. fine
9 .. W N.E. fine morng - showery — Dodson left
10 .. W S.E. fine frosty.
11 .. W S.E. morng fine
12 .. W N.E. fine - afternoon showery
13 .. W N.E. fine.
14 S. .. W N.E. fine.
15 .. W N.E. fine
16 .. W S.E. fine — — — Sir Wolstans birth day.
17 .. W S.E. dark & rough morng, rain —
18 .. W S.W. windy & showery. — —
19 .. W S.W. fine & warm — —
20 .. W S.W. fine — — —
21 S. .. W S.W. morng wet, afternoon fine —
22 .. W S.W. dark & damp - wet & stormy — Knaggs head [illegible]
23 .. W S. dark, rain & storm —
24 .. W S. stormy - very wet —
25 .. W S.W. very wet —
26 .. W W. fair & sunny - light showers —
27 .. W S.W. drizzling day - Eveng fine —
28 S. .. W N.W. very fine —
29 .. W S. dark day - cold but fine, W.N.W. at night.
30 .. W S.W. fine — — — — Mr. Garforth died about 2 a. m.
31. .. W S.W. dark & showery.

November

1st W S.W. dark morng - fine — — Garforth [illegible]
2 W.S. fine.
3 W.S.W. fine & frosty
4 S W.S.W. showery.
W.S.W. showers. W.N.W. thunder.
5 W.S.W. snow showers, - W.N.W. thunder
6 W.S.W. snow & frosty, wet & stormy.
7 W.N.W. snow & frosty, wet & stormy.
8 W.S.W. rain & wind.

9 w, SW - Rain & mist.
10 w, SW - dull & damp
11 S w, SW, very wet.
12 w, SW, dark & damp.
13 w, SW - morng fine, showers. — Went to see Wm Walker - Robt Wilson called.
14 w, SW - dark & showers.
15 w, NW - fine morngs - evng fine — Thanksgiving day.
16 w, NW - fine.
17 w, SW, lowering morng. Rain
18 S w, NW - rain. — Tea at Dalehead.
19 w, NW - fine
20 w, SW, - misty
21 w, SW - fine but dark — Heads hounds arrived
22 w, SW - misty. wet — Shepherds feast
23 w SW - very wet
24 w, NW, fine morng.
25 S w, SW, fair, showers. w, N w.
26 w, NW, frost & mist - night frosty
27 w, NW, hard frost.
28 w, SW frost.
29 w, SW, frost & snow & windy night wet.
30 w, SW fine & freezing - thaw, - rain. — St Andrew's day.

December

1 w, SW, fair. cold Evening. fine night — called to Harry.
2 S w, SW wet — Advent Sunday, Rounding
3 w, NE - fair, very cold
4 w, NE - frost - snow, slight.
5 w, SE, hard frost - snow thaw
6 w, SW - wind & rain
7 w, SE - dry & cold
8 w, S - wet
9 S w, SW, fine & mild
10 w, SW - misty — went to Keswick saw Kembley.
11 w, NE. fine
12 w, SE - frost — Mary Wilson, married
13 w, SE - frost - windy - sleet at night
14 w, SE - mild.
... mild wet

16 S w, SW. fair rain
17 w, SW - rain
18 w, SW - rain, w, N w.
19 w, N - fine — Mary Walkers feast.
20 w, N - fine -
21 w, N - slight frost
22 w, N - light snow & frost — Xmas market at Keswick.
23 S w, N - frost & fine
24 w, NW - fine - Dodson arrived — John Atkinson married
25 Xm w, NW - fine
26 w, NW - fine - living w, N.
27 w, N - fine, slight frost
28 w, N - frost & slight showers
29 w, NE - frost — Dodson left.
30 S w, NE - frost
31 w, NE. frost — [illegible]

I may observe That the accts from the Continent represented the Weather as Unusually Severe.

Diary for 1830.

Wind & weather to the 9 point

1 .. W N E – January – frost continues fine & strong
2 .. W S W – slack & thaw.
3 .. W SW – thaw & misty.
4 .. W SW – wind & showers.
5 .. W SW – snow & hail. W NW, snow showers.
6 S. W SW frost. — — — — — Epiphany.
7 .. W N – fine & frost.
8 .. W W – fine & frosty D. Thwaite took tea with us. — at Keswick
9 .. W SW do.
10 .. W S. cloudy – betokens snow.
11 .. W SW – do. but no snow as yet, only a little sprinkling, melting again
12 .. W SE – SE, cloudy for snow
13 S. W E. fine. — — — — not one person at Church
14 .. W E – do
15 .. W E – fine, more snow fallen.
16 .. W E. thick snowy looking day. — — — my little girl born at Eglesthwaite.
17 .. W NE – beautiful day.
18 .. W S E. dark day. sleet.
19 .. W E – snowy looking – thaw
20 S. W SE – fine & frost — — — — Baby died
21 .. W E do – — — — baby buried
22 .. W SE – – SW – thaw — thaw
23 .. W SW – thaw
24 .. W SW – thaw.
25 .. W SW – rain – west – fine – mild
26 .. W N W – showery – stormy. – freezing again
27 S. W N – hard frost – W, E. likely for snow – rain
28 .. W SW – showery.
29 .. W NE – fine & bright — Mother had never arrived before 6 at night.
30 .. W SW – fine
31. .. W SE – frost & windy.

Note that the word fine expresses fair in this book.

February

1 W S W – rain – W west – fine
2 W SW – showers rain & wind
3 S W, W. fine – Sexagesima
4 W, SW fine – Crossket at ...Gate, Crag & Bields
5 W, SW fine but cold ... very well.
6 W – N W – rough morng – high wind.
7 W – N W – fine
8 W – N W – cold
9 W, SW – very stormy
10 S W, NW – snow & rain. Quinquages. afterwards fine — One year this day I preached first at Wythburn.
11 W, SW – rain. snow – W, N W. fine
12 W, N. fine, frosty.
13 W, N W – frost. Ash Wednesday – Went to Carlisle
14 W, SW – showery — Arrived at the Dales.
15 W, SW – showers — Returned from Carlisle
16 W – S – rain
17 S W, SW – rainy – should be lent. — Thrushes singing.
18 W, SW – misty & rain.
19 W, SW – do
20 W, W – fine & sunny.
21 W – N W – rain – high wind.
22 W. N W. fair, but windy. — Birds whistling.
23 W, SW – very spring like —
24 S W – SW – fine, mild – 2 Sund in Lent. — My wife at Wythburn
25 W, SW fine but cold — mild
26 W, SW, very fine.
27 W – SW, fine – evening W, SE. — Saw a bat for 9th time this season
28 W – W – fine but hazy.

March

1 w, W, fine. — wagtail arrived & yellow Hammer

2 w, SW; fair but cold & misty

3 S w, SW-West - very wet - Evg - fine 3rd Sund in Lent

4 w, NE. fair but cold. — Rheuben breaking up ye meadow in front of Kings Head.

5 w, SW. fair but cloudy - damp - wet.

6 w, SW fine — Hickens boy Wread. James Thorpe married at Cadoby.

7 w, SW fine

8 w, SW very fine

9 w, SW fine but chill.

10 S w, NW - fine but cold - 4th Sund in Lent. Good congregatn

11 W. N very fine

12 w, N - very fine & warm — My wife & boy went to Keswick.

13 w, N - very fine morng —

14 w, NW - fine - mild — Head's hounds killed a Martin or Mare.

15 w, NE - very fine.

16 w, NE - fine - but chill. — Removed to Armboth

17 S w, NE - fine - very mild - 5th Sund in Lent.

18 w, N - fine & warm — Sheep delivered at ye Kings Head.

19 w, N - very fine - — Mr Westray's sale & fight.

20 w, N - very fine. — Crosker's hounds killed a fox in Grasmere.

21 w, N - fine but cold -

22 w, NW - fine but cold.

23 w, N - frost & Snow - fine but cold.

24 S w, NW. fine but cold - 6 Sund in Lent. hard frost at night - Severer than during the winter

25 w, NW - very fine, but cold. at night a fall of Snow.

26 w, W - very fine.

27 w, NE, very fine - frost at night.

28 w, N - very fine - ditto -

29 w, NW - fine.

30 w, SW; cold, windy & light snow showers.

31 S - Easter, w, SW - fine but hazy — A few Easter tourists on the road.

w, SW - fine.

w, S fine - fished Red Tarn - nil.

fine -

— very hot weather + Mrs Skelton thrown out of a gig on Wm Latter, on the first of June.

1 month.

April

1 w, SW windy & showery — — Went to see Miss Skelton [illegible] fished for ye first time. nil

2 w, SW - fine & mild — —

3 w, SW - showers -

4 w, SW - wet & mild - — fished for ye 2d time - nil Jos: Westray breaking up ye great field.

5 w, W. fair but cloudy -

6 w, SW fine spring weather.

7 S w, SW - very wet morning.

8 w, S. very fine - — night cold.

9 w, S. cold

10 w, SW - wet morng - afterwards very fine. funeral at the Cherrytree

11 w, SW - very fine - warm

12 w, SW - very fine & sunny day.

13 w, SE, fine - warm -

14 S w, SE - fine, warm

15 w, SE - cloudy & cold showers - springlike.

16 w, SW - showers - Evening fine.

17 w, NW - showers, but mild — Mary Wilson died

18 w, W - fine - a lovely spring, so far.

19 w, S, very wet, - fine from noon

20 w, W, very wet morning. — Mary Wilson buried

21 S w, NW fine, Evening wind N - fine

22 w, NW; very fine.

23 w, NW - very fine. Evening, SW. Mrs Westray went to Cockermouth for the fair.

24 w, N. fine - Evening W, SW.

25 w, SW - very wet.

26 w, SE. fine.

27 w, SE. fine - cold

28 S w, E - fine - cold winds.

29 w, NE - fine, cold.

30 w, NE - fine but cold. —

A fine springlike month.

The wild fowl which wintered on Thirlmere left it about the begining of this month - Two large ducks, called shell ducks remain & appear to have made their Nest on a small isla

March

1 w, W, fine. — wagtail yellow
2 w, SW; fair but cold & misty
3 S w, SW- wet - very wet - Eng. T.
4 w, NE- fine but cold.
5 w, SW- fair but clear
6 w, SW- fine

May

1 w- NE; fine but very cold. — Mr Dodson arrived at Armboth
2 w, NE. very fine. — cuckoo first heard and swallows seen
3 w, N. fine - went to Rackwell falls. Return of St Johns saw swallows, a flock, a fortnight before.
4 w, NW- fine - with hail showers
5 S w, NE. heavy showers of snow. cold.
6 w, NE- very fine, but cold.
7 w, NE- fine but cold.
8 w, NW- very fine - mild. — Rain in Leicestershire. Dodson's Fair. Thorpe's letter.
9 w, NW- very fine — Ascension day.
10 w, SW- very wet
11 w, W- very fine — fished St John's with Dodson. Fair sport.
12 S w, W- fine, quarrelled with my wife.
13 w, NW- very fine. went to Honister Crag with Dodson
14 w, NW- showers.
15 w, NE fine but cold
16 w, NW- mild
17 w, W- Bright & fine
18 w, S. very mild and fine. Whitsaturday.
19 S w, S. lovely day "growing weather". Whitsunday.
20 w, S. showery morning.
21 w, SE. very fine. Legberthwaite sports.
22 w, SE. very fine — heavy Rain at Keswick & Threlkeld
23 w, E. fine. thunder & showers.
24 w, S.E. fine - warm
25 w, S. showery.
26 S w, S very wet. fine growing day.
27 w, S. fine - fished Wythburn Heads - fair sport
28 w, S.
29 w, S. fine - fished Red Tarn - nil.
30 w, S. fine -
31 w, S. fine - very hot weather + — Miss Skelton thrown out of a gig on Wm Cutter on the ford of June.

A lovely month.

June

1 S w- SW. very fine +
2 S w, SW. very fine
3 w, SW- fine — went to see Miss Skelton
4 w, SW- fine, showers in morning. — Scarcely any tourists as yet.
5 w, SW- showery fine morning.
6 w, SW- wet afternoon - fair evening. — The bracken clock are in great abundance. Fished Wythburn again fine sport
7 w, W. showers, afterwards wet night.
8 w, W, fair - NW
9 S w, SW, fair good congregation 56. — few tourists hitherto.
10 w, SW- very fine - Miss Skelton & Mrs Brougham came to see us.
11 w, S. cloudy.
12 w, SW- very wet morning & Evening. — fine growing weather so far.
13 w, W. wet day.
14 w, S. Morning showery. Evg. very wet.
15 w, SW. fine. went to Keswick. — saw Kembley at Keswick
16 S w, SW- fine - good congregation, about 50.
17 w, S, fair, but cloudy. Every thing looks promising for farmers
18 w, SW- fine and warm — Geo Wilson's sheep washing
19 w, SW- fine.
20 w, S. fine. Mr Dodson left Armboth. — Dalehead sheep washing.
21 w, S. fair but cloudy. Evening wet. — cuckoo still strong in voice
22 w, SW showery. Evening fair
23 S w N W fine — good congregation
24 w, W- very fine - Mist on the mountains - went to Lazonby, found I missed my brother as he was
25 w W- very fine. sultry & hazy.
26 w NW- fine
27 w NW- fine - Visitation at Penrith — Came home. Cuckoo gone, not heard since the Monday 24th.
28 w N W. fair & fine.
29 w W- fine but cold & cloudy.
30 S. w S. cloudy - showery - very wet. good congregation.

July

1 w. SW- morning fine but cold - Evening wet.
2 w, SW- fine but cloudy & cold. wet night. Miss Lawson came
3 w, W. showers - fine, but cloudy. Lake water over the pathway.
4 w, W. fair but cloudy. Evening bright.

5 w, W. cold & showery.
6 w, NW. wet. went to Keswick — — Miss Lawson left us.
7 S w, N. cold but fair – Evenig fine.
8 w, N. very fine — — Geo: Wilson's clipping
9 w, NW. Misty rain — — Dalehead clipping
10 w, NW fine.
11 w, NW. fair & sultry, but cloudy. T. Wightman's clipping.
12 w, NW fair, sultry & misty.
13 w, SE. fine.
14 S w, SE. fine. moderate congregation.
15 w, SE. fine.
16 w, SE. morng fine – Evenig fine. Mrs L. & Bazz went to Keswick
17 w, S. morng fine & Evenig showers.
18 w, SW. fair, sultry & misty.
19 w, SW. fair but cloudy.
20 • w, N. lovely day — — — Mr Harting left our lodgings
21 S w, S. beautiful weather, – sact Sunday. Good congregation – 16 Com'ts
22 w, SE. lovely day.
23 w, SE. very fine. — — Evenig wet.
24 w, SW. wet.
25 w, E. Showers.
26 w, NE Showers.
27 w, N. Morng fair – fair.
28 S w, NE. fine. — — — average congregation.
29 w, N. fine.
30 w, N. fine — — Miss Rawthwell's came to Wdd's Ahead.
31 w, SW. misty & cloudy.
an average congregation; 20 full grown persons.

August.

1 w, SW. fine — finished hay.
2 w, SW. fine – misty & cloudy afternoon.
3 w, SW. [illegible] fine.
4 S w, S. very wet. — — Little Westray 2/ [illegible]
5 w, W. showery. — Evenig wet. Mr Rhodes & family left
6 w, NW. fine — — finished lythburn – 20 L.
7 w, SW. fine – finished the hay.
8 w, NW. wet.
9 w, NW. wet.
10 w, W. fine.
11 S w, S. wet — — average congregation
12 w, NE. showery [illegible] fine Eveng

13 w, NE. very fine — — — went to Wast Head with Bazz & Mama
14 w, NE fine.
15 w, N. fine.
16 w, N. fine
17 w, N. fine.
18 S w, SW. wet – Evenig fair. very mod: congregation
19 w, SW. showery.
20 w, W. Showery
21 w, NW. showery morng – fine
22 w, SW. showery. — Collgate at lythburn robbed when John Hawkrigg lost his shirt and shoes – &c
23 w, SW fine
24 w, SW showery.
25 S w, SW a storm of wind and rain could not get to Chapel.
26 w, NW. showers – fine.
27 w, S. very wet.
28 w, NW. fine
29 w, NW. fine.
30 w, N. fine
31 w, SW fair.
An indifferent & cold month.

September

1 S w, NW. misty – Sultry. mod: congregation
2 w, NW. fine, but cloudy.
3 w, NW, cloudy.
4 w, NW. very fine.
5 w, NW. very fine. — — Threlkeld fair – J. Westray began to reap his oats.
6 w, NE. fine but cold.
7 w, E. fine.
8 S w, NE. fine misty the morning. — very good congregation
9 w, NE. fine – misty morng.
10 w, SE. fine – very misty in y morng.
11 w, SE. fine.
12 w, S. fine — — — went to St Johns with my wife —
13 w, S fine —
14 w, S fine – very hot.
15 S w, S. fine but cloudy. — — good congregation
16 w, SE. fine –
17 w, S. fine, but cloudy.
18 w, S. fine – cloudy or murky.
19 w, S. fine – ditto.
20 w, S. Misty – Showers – Evig fine.
21 w, SW. showery day.

22 S w, SW - showers. — Mod: Congregation.
23 w, S. Fair & Sultry.
24 w, SW - fine.
25 w, S, fine.
26 w, SW, showers. — took tea with Nancy Dan[illegible]
27 w, SW, showers.
28 w, SW, showers. — Jane Atkinson confined at the Kings Head.
29 S w, SW - showers — Mod: Congregation.
30. w, NW, fine with occas. showers. — Crosthws hounds out at Ley [illegible]

October.

1 w. N. fine but cold.
2 w, NE. fine.
3 w, SE. fine
4 w, SW, showers
5 w, W, showers
6 S w, SW. morng fair - afternoon wet, — Average Congregation
7 w, NW. very stormy, - Cake light the hitherto.
8 w. N. fine Mrs Westray went to Cockermouth
9 w, NW. fine
10 w, N, fine — slight snow on Helvellyn
11 w, NE fine
12 w, NE - fine
13 S w, NW - misty rain — average congregation
14 w, NW - fine
15 w, W - fine
16 w, W showery
17 w, W. fine
18 w, W. slight showers.
19 w. W. showery Mrs W. returned from Cockermouth
20 S w. N. fine — thin congregation
21 w, NE - fine
22 w. SW. fine - Eveng showers.
23 w - NE - fair.
24 w. NE. Snow on ye mountains - first day of winter
25 w. NE - fine but cold.
26 w, N - fine.
27 S w, SW - morng fine - Eveng wet — thin congregation
28 w - NW - fine.
29 w, NW - fine
30 w, NW - fine.
31. w, NW. showery - afternoon - fine.

1st w. W. wet. — Kings Head hunt.
2 w. W. wet — Tup fair at Keswick.
3 S w. W - fair & fine. — thin congregation.
4 w, W - showers
5 w. W - showers — dined at Dalehead with the Suttons. Mrs Westray went to Cockermouth
6 w. W - showers.
7 w. SW - showers & high wind
8 w. NW, - showers.
9 w. W - fair but damp.
10 S w. SW - fair but dark — Sabbath Congregation.
11 w, W - very wet.
12 w, NW very fine
13 w, NW - fair but dark
14 w, NW - hard frost - lovely day. — Mrs Westray returned. Cockermouth Church burnt.
15 w, NW - Misty morng — fine
16 w, NW - Misty - rain — 1/2 yrs Salary due.
17 S w, NW - fine — {Average congregation half years Salary due.
18 w, W. misty with Slight Showers.
19 w, S. very stormy - wind & rain.
20 w, W - fine - Misty - rain
21 w, SW - fair - very fine
22 w, SW - misty. damp
23 w, SW - misty - rain - fair — {went to Keswick received salary
24 S w, SW very wet - went to Wythburn - but no congregation,
25 w, W. fair — floods out
26 w, NW - fine — Crosthws dogs at Armth
27 w, NW - frost - Snow on ye fells - fine
28 w. N. frost - very fine — Mr Lawson taken suddenly ill.
29 w, S. hard frost.
30 w, S - hard frost - beautiful weather.

December.

1 S w - SE - hard frost - very fine — Small congregation
2 w. S. wet.
3 w, S. fine
4 w, W; Showers - fine
5 w, SW. wet and misty.
6 w, SW. fine.
7 w, S. fine.
8 S w. S - fine — Average Congregation

9 w. S. frost - fine.
10 w. S. frost - fine.
11 w. S. fine --- Eving wet.
12 w. W. fine
13 w. S. misty and windy -
14 w. S. dark - squally day.
15 S w. W. dark & cold but fine. --- Average Congregation
16 w. NW. fine & cold.
17 w. W. Changable - showers, hail &c
18 w. W. hard frost - very fine - Snow on ye fells.
19 w. NE. hard frost - very fine.
20 w. N. frost - lovely weather.
21 w. W. Showers
22 S w. W. fine ——— --- Average Congregation
23 w. W. fine
24 w. NW fine —— Showers
25 Xmas w. NW. fine —— ——— 11 Communicants
26 w. W. fine
27 w. W. Showery.
28 w. W. showers
29 S w. W. fine morning - Showers ——— Average Congregation -
30 w. SW. wet —— Eving fine —— {Xmas party at Trespath. Mrs Westray went to Bakermouth. 4th time in 12 months
31. w. S. wet.

1851.

January.

1 w. W. fair - Lake very high
2 w. W. fair after a night of fearful wind & rain. *The road torn up between Brotty & Stoney bridges & in other places. The brook rushed thro the Kings Head the night before. The inhabitants obliged to take refuge in the upper apartments. A chasm formed in ye road at Raven Crag.
3 w. W. fine.
4 w. W. fine --- very wet night.
5 S w. SW. fine - Small Congregation.
6 w. SW. frosty morning - very fine
7 w. SW. Misty - with showers.
8 w. SW. misty -
9 w. W. fine - Snow during the night.
10 w. S. wet
11 w. SW. showers - night very wet
12 S w. S. fair. Mrs W-y came home. Thin congregation 7 persons
13 w. S. wet
14 w. S. wet
15 w. S. showers - very wet --- went to Wythburn for Register
16 w. S. very wet - nothing but floods. ——— [illegible]
17 w. S. hail - thunder & lightening
18 w. S fair.
19 S w. S. wet —— 7 persons at Chapel.
20 w. S. wet
21 w. SW. wet - fair - hail showers - Snow on ye fells
22 w. SW. wet - hail & sleet.
23 w. S. fine
24 w. SW. showers -
25 w. SW. hail - rain - sleet - snow on ye fells.
26 S w. SW. wet - sleety - fine - rain - no Congregation.
27 w. W. fine - ---
28 w. SW. fair ——— rain -
29 w. SW. very stormy.
30 w. W. hail and sleet - Snow.
31. w. NE. Hard frost.

February.

1 w. N. fine —— -- frosty.
2 S SW. heavy fine -- frosty — ° Thin Congregation
3 w. E. heavy Snow.
4 w. NW. frost. --- thaw.
5 w. SW. heavy rain --- snow gone
6 w. W. fine
7 w. W. wet.
8 w. NW. fine
9 S w. W. fine. ——— improved Congregation
10 w. W. misty
11 w. W. fine
12 w. W. fine
13 w. SE. fine —— went to Ambleside.
14 w. W. fine
15 w. W. fine -
16 S w. S. fine ——— - improved Congregation
17 w. W. fine
18 w. SW. wet
19 w. SW. wet ——— Eving fair
20 w. SW. fine - frosty --- Geldart's Hounds in Wythburn.
21 w. W. fine - frosty
22 w. NW. fine - frosty
23 S w. SW. fine - frosty —— thin Congregation.

Lovely weather

Lovely weather

24 w, SW - fine - frosty - w NW. — {fine last two days
Cutting timber.
25 w, NE - fine - windy.
26 w, NE - fine frosty - ——— Crosher at Wythburn
27 w, NE - fine - frosty.
28 w.

22 fine days - this month

March

1 w, N - fine
2 S w, N - fine — Congregation Small
3 w, W - fine but cloudy.
4 w, W - fine - SW - rainy - NW.
5 w, NW - fine - Ash wednesday — only John Banks at Chapel.
6 w, N. fine - cold
7 w, SW - fine - frosty
8 w, SW - fine - very cold
9 S w, S. very cold - sleet &c — thin Congregation
10 w, NW - fine but cold.
11 w, S - NW - fine
12 w, SW - fine — {at Keswick - &c
13 w, SW - fine — Mrs L. & Baggy at Keswick
14 w, SW - Showers & cold
15 w, W - Showers - fine.
16 S w, NE - fine. — better Congregation
17 w, SW - fine - misty - showers
18 w, NW - Showers
19 w, SW - fine
20 w, SW - showers - fine.
21 w, SW - showers - fine

Mild and Spring like

22 w, SW - Showers -
23 S w, N showers — beautiful Evening. — Mod: Congregation - a Subs - for the Soc - prop. Gos - 1/1 - One Shilling and One Penny!!!!
24 w, NW - showers.
25 w, SW - fine - mild - cloudy - showers.
26 w, W - wet
27 w, SW - cloudy but fair — Showers.
28 w, W - fine — Keswick.
29 w, NW - fine. — Keswick.
30 S w, NW - fine ... showers. — Congregation improved
31 w, NW - fair ... showers - cold.

21 fine days.

April

1 w, S. fine - mild.
2 w, NW - showers - cold
3 w, NW - fine -
4 w, NW - fine - cold
5 w, SW - fine - cold
6 S w, S. fine ... mild — Mod: Congregation
7 w, SW, fine ... warm — went to Penrith
8 w, SW - fine - mild - went to Crangle dyke - Wilson better
9 w, NE - fine ... went to Carlisle
10 w, E. fine - cold
11 w, E - fine - cold - returned to Penrith on my road Home
12 w, E. fine -
13 S w, E - fine - Palm Sunday. — {thin poor Congregation
read myself in.
14 w, E - fine - cold
15 w, E - fine - cold
16 w, E - fine - cold
17 w, SE - fine - mild
18 w, SW - good friday - cold - cold — + good attendance at the Communion.
19 w, SW - showers - cold
20 S w, S. fine Easter day, warm — + heard the cuckoo 1st time this season
21 w, S - fine - but windy - fished St Johns — killed One. Mr Hardisty - One.
22 w, S. fine - warm
23 w, S. lovely day.
24 w, W. beautiful - thunder - went to Raven Crag with Adam (potatoes planted).
25 w, N. very fine -
26 w, N - hail & snow - very cold.
27 S w, N - fine - hail showers - stormy. — thin Congregation
28 w, NE - moist morning - snow
29 w, NE fine - very cold.
30 w, N - fine ... fine. — went to Keswick. saw Mr Wilson

For May, vide 4 p's forward.

May 1851.

winterly weather

1 w. NW. fine - warm
2 w. NE. fine - cold - hail & snow showers.
3 w. N. fine but cold - snow showers.
4 S w. NE. fine - cold - snow showers ---- thin Congregation
5 w. N. snow showers.
6 w. N. fine - warm
7 w. W. fine -- warm - growing weather
8 w. S. mild rain -- do.
9 w. SE mild rain. fished Leythburn with Mr. Hardisty. - 0.
10 w. SE. fine -
11 S w. NE. fair but cold - ---------- thin Congregation
12 w. NE. fine - mild
13 w. E. fine - warm
14 w. E. fine - warm
15 w. SW fine -- warm -
16 w. S. fine cloudy - mild
17 w. S. fine - very warm
18 S w. W. showers - rain - very fine - --- thin Congregation -
19 S w. NW. hail showers - very cold - thunder
20 w. NW. fine but cold
21 w. NW. fine - warm - frosty at night
22 w. W. fine - warm - do
23 w. W. fine - warm
24 w. W. fine - cloudy -
25 S w. W. fair - cloudy - showers Good Congregation - 35.
26 w. W. fine - cold - showers
27 w. W. fine - showers
28 w. W. fine - warm fished ye Lake with Messrs. Pratt & Hardisty. 0
29 w. NW. fine - Ascension day --- John Banks at chapel.
30 w. W. fine - hot.
31 w. W. fine - hot - Raing cool & cloudy.

June

1 - S w. NW. very warm - cloudy.
2 w. W. fine, cloudy,
3 w. W. dark - showers. Mr. Godson - arrived -
4 w. NW. very fine - snow on all ye hills. went to Tongue with Joh[n]

5 w. SW. very wet - fine
6 w. SW. fine fished Leythburn .. 15. with Mr. Godson
7 w. SW. fine
8 S w. W. showers .... Whitsunday -- thin Congn. 8 Communicts
9 w. W. fine - mild
10 w. NW dark showery Morning ... fine
11 w. NW. fine
12 w. S - very wet.
13 w. SW - very fine. fished Leythburn .. 5.
14 w. S. very fine -- went to Newlands
15 S w. S. very wet - Trinity Sunday - - poor Congregation. 7 Communicts.
16 w. W. showers & cold --- fine.
17 w. NW. very fine --- mild -
18 w. W. showers. cold.
19 w. SW. fine - showers - mild rain.
20 w. SW. showers & mild..
21 w. SW. lovely day - rain - thunder
22 S w. W. fine - showers - ~~fine~~ - Good Congregation 39.
23 w. NW. fine - but cool.
24 w. W. fine - cloudy but warm
25 w. W. misty and slight showers.
26 w. SW. very fine - Dr. Thwaite washed the sheep
27 w. SW. very fine & sultry.
28 w. SW. do -
29 w. S. do - very sultry - Splendid - Good Congregation 34
30 w. S. do - --- Heard the Cuckoo last, on Sunday

Splendid weather

July.

1 w. S. fine summer weather - thunder showers. - Cockermouth races
2 w. E. fine & sunny.
3 w. E. fine - sunny but cold for ye season -
4 w. E. fine --- wind westering ye Evening.
5 w. NW. fine - - - Adam Wilkinson & ... fell
6 S w. NW. fine but cloudy - ------ Good Congregation 41.
7 w. NW. fair but misty - & south - west.
8 w. NW wet - wet - would have been the Dalehead dipping.
9 w. NW. fair - SW. - fair - slight showers.
10 w. NW. showers.
11 w. SW. fine.
12 w. SW. slight showers - wet Evening -
13 S w. SW. wet morning - stormy. -- thin Congregation. John

14 w, SW. very wet & stormy.
15 w, SW changeable. — fine
16 w, NW. fine – slight showers. Geo: Wilson's clipping.
17 w, SW. fine
18 w, SW. fine.
19 w, SW. fine – cloudy. wet; repaired the Man on Fisher Crag with Messrs Dodson and Hardisty.
20 S w, SW. wet. Congregation 18.
21 w, W. fair but cold & cloudy. — Saw a cuckoo in ye Park when in company with Messrs H. & Dodson, – no mistake.
22 w, W. fine – very warm – wet.
23 w, E. very fine.
24 w, NE. fine but cloudy.
25 w, NW. fine but cloudy.
26 w, W. very fine – Mr & Mrs Gandy & family pic nic'd.
27 S w, W. fine – Congregation 29.
28 w, SW. wet – Showers.
29 w, SW. fine –
30 w, S. very fine – sultry
31 w, SW. wet — wet — John Banks called.

August.

1 w, SW. fine – Sultry
2 w, SW. fine – Sultry
3 S w, S. wet & Sultry — wet — — Small Congregation 16.
4 w, W. fine morning
5 w, SE. fine – Lovely day.
6 w, SE. Lovely – very warm
7 w, E. beautiful weather
8 w, E. very fine — Old Wm Wilson taken ill.
9 w, E. very fine
10 S w, NE cloudy but fine. — — Good Congregation. 80
11 w, SE. cloudy – fair – slight rain.
12 w, S. cloudy and Sultry – Wm Wilson died.
13 w, S. do
14 w, S. wet — Evening fine.
15 w, SW – fine — Mr & Mrs Gelbanks visited us.
16 w, S. fine —
17 S w, S. Showers – afternoon NE – good Congregation 33.
18 w, NE – fine
19 w, SW – cloudy
20 w, SW – cloudy – Showers
21 w, S. wet and windy
22 w, S wet — Showers — Adam Started for London –
23 w, W, Showers.
24 S w, very wet — fine — Congregation 28
25 w, NW. fine — went to West Head, – to tea
26 w, S very wet –
27 w, W. fine but cold
28 w, NW – fine but cold.
29 w, NW – rain at night – morning fine.
30 w, N. fine – J. W. began to reap. Adam returned from London.
31 S w, N. fine good Congregation. 98. Commenced the Prayer for fine weather – which was repeated the 3 following Sundays.

A dismal month.

September.

1 w, W. fine but cloudy.
2 w, SW. wet — Evening fine.
3 w, NW. fine – very fine.
4 w, NW – fine. Threlkeld fair – Mr Dodson left and took up his qrs at the Kings Head.
5 w, NE. fine. cool but ...
6 w, E. fine. but cool.
7 S w, E. fine but cloudy – Good Congregation. 48.
8 w, E. fine but cloudy.
9 w, SE. fine – hot. — Mary Cole & Sarah Walker tea'd with us.
10 w, S. fine – do – hot. ~~The ... from~~
11 w, S fine – hot. The Girls from West head tea'd with us.
12 w, S. fine.
13 w, S. Sublime weather.
14 S w, S. fine. — Congregation 29.
15 w, SW – fine visited Lyddy Hind – Mrs W. let her lodgings.
16 w, SW. fine. — — J. Wilson finished reaping.
17 w, S. fine.
18 w, N. fine – ~~...~~
19 w, N. fine – cloudy.

21 S w, SE, fine - Congregation 37. Mrs E. went to Cockermouth.
22 w, Sw, fine morning - Evening showers
23 w, NW - fine wintry but misty. Miss Clindes left.
24 w S - fine but misty -
25 w, N - very wet - Snow on Helvellyn -
26 w, N - wet - Snow on ye fells
27 w, N - Showers - went to Keswick
28 S w, W - fine - Congregation 30.
29 w, SW, fine but cloudy
30 w, S - very wet -

October -

1 w, S. fair but cold and windy - night very wet.
2 w, S - fine - showers & thunder - fine
3 w, S - fair but misty. Wm Morley started for London.
4 w, S. fine -
5 S w, NW - Showers - 12 Communicants -
6 w, NW, fine - Showers.
7 w, W, Showery - cold
8 w, S fine
9 w, S - Misty & wet.
10 w, W, fine.
11 w, W. Showers - Swallows: ~~[illegible]~~.
12 S w, SW, fine - Congregation 28.
13 w, SE - very wet.
14 w, W - fine - wet. *Swallows not gone
15 w, W - fair — showers - The family left Dalehead.
16 w, NW - fine.
17 w, NW, - fine - Slight showers.
18 w, S - misty and rainy. Swallows gone.
19 S w, S - wet - Congregation 19.
20 w, S - fine - misty.
21 w, S - fair - but misty.
22 w, S - fine -
23 w, S - fine - lovely weather.
24 w, S - fine - Old Nancy D - first told me that she had made her will.
25 w, S. fine
26 S w, SE - fine - small Congregation
27 w, NW - fine
28 w, W - fine but cloudy - wet night
29 w NW fine - Showers. —

30 w, N - showers and stormy
31 w, NW, fine but snow like.

November -

1 w, NW - Showers
2 S w, NW - fine - Mod. Congregation -
3 w, NW - frost & fine. Snow on the fells. Croshers
4 w, NW, frost - fine - dog at Wythburn.
5 w, NW - frost - fine.
6 w, N. frost fine
7 w, NW - fine but thawing.
8 w, SW - misty & slight rain. Martin was jailed at Keswick*
9 S w, N: fair - Small Congregation (Mrs Westray left Wythburn)
10 w, NW - fair
11 w, NW - fine
12 w, NW - fine
13 w, NW - fair -
14 w, NW - fine
15 w, NW fine
16 S w, N - fine frost - Mod Cong^n.
17 w, N - fine frost - Stove came to Wythburn
18 w, N - do -
19 w, SW - slight Snow
20 w, N. fine frost - Mrs Westray returned.
21 w, NW fine - put up the Stove.
22 w, N - frost and fine
23 S w, SW - soft and cloudy - Congregation mod. 23.
24 w, W - fine
25 w, SW - fine - SE. frosty.
26 w, E. fine - frosty
27 w, N. fine. — Kings Head hunt -
28 w, N frost and fine
29 w, NE fine & frost - cloudy.
30. S w, NE - fine - E. frost - Congregation 21

A fine month

Dec.

1 w, SW. cloudy – thaw – fine & frost.
2 w, N. frost & fine
3 w, W. thaw – but fair
4 w, NW. fine
5 W, NW. fine
6 w, W. Showers.
7 S w, SW. wet. Congregation 5 – adults.
8 w, W. fine but windy.
9 w, S. dark & moist day – wet.
10 w, SW. wet. very wet.
11 w, SW. fine & cloudy.
12 w, SW. fine.
13 w, S. very fine.
14 S w, S. fine & frost. Congregation – 39.
15 w, S. misty – fine.
16 w, S. misty – fine.
17 w, S. misty —
18 w, S. misty – rain at night
19 w, S. misty
20 w, S. misty with showers.
21 S w, W. fine. Congregat[io]n small.
22 w, W. fine – Lovely day.
23 w, SE. very fine – white frost.
24 w, S. fine but dark and cold
25 Xtms day w, SW. fine but dark & cold – 8 Communicants.
26 w, SW. fine morning.
27 w, W. fine.
28 S w, N. fine – Congregation 23.
29 w, W. fine – W. J. Atkinson's Xmas feast.
30. w, W. fine – Mrs W. went to Cockermouth
31. w, E. fine.

Severe weather on [the] Continent – Heavy Sn[ow]

Jany. 1852.

1 w, W. fine
2 w, NW. fine
3 W. w, E. very wet.
4 S w, NW. very fine – Mod: Congregation
5 w, W. stormy.
[6]
7 w, W. Stormy – Thos Weyhtman &c tail with us.
8 w, SW. Stormy. – heavy fall of Snow at night.
9 w, NW. dark snowy looking morning.
10 w, W. hard frost.
11 S w, NE. Snowy – No Service at Wythburn – no one there.
12 w, SW. very wet
13 w, NW. frost & fine.
14 w, SW. Showers & cold – Reuben & John A. played a rubber at Wth.
15 w, SW. wet.
16 w, W. fine
17 w, NW. fine – showers.
18 S w, S. very fine. Congregation 21 – adults.
19 w, S. dark and drizzling.
20 w, SW, Showers & cold —
21 w, W. showers – cold – very wet.
22 w, W. showers – cold –
23 w, W, fine – but cloudy
24 w, W. very wet and stormy
25 S w, SW. showery – indifft Congregation
26 w, SW, Showers & cold.
27 w, W. stormy.
28 w, NW, fine.
29 w, N. wet.
30 w, NW, wet & stormy.
31 – w, SW, cloudy – showery.

Considerable apprehensions of invasion by the French.

February.

1 S w, NW. stormy – thin Congregation
2 w, SW, tempestuous – Stormy and heavy flood.
3 w, SW, fine – mild – hail & thunder
4 w, S. very stormy.
5 w, W. cloudy & damp.
6 w, W. slight showers – mild.

7 w. n w. - Slight showers - fine but cold
8 S w. w. wet - small Congregation - 7.
9 w. n w. Morng fine - snow -
10 w. n w. - fine.
11 w. S w. fine frosty.
12 w. S w. cold & mizzling Rain
13 w. S w. cold & mizzling.
14 w. S w. fine.
15 S w. w. - Showers - fine - Congregation 18.
16 w. n w. Fair but blustering
17 w. n w. wet - & cloudy
18 w. n w. very fine but cold, frosty - Note, the weather took up on this day.
19 w. n w. fine but cold - frost.
20 w. n. - fine - cold and frost.
21 w. n w. - fine - frost.
22 S w. n. - fine - Congregation 27
23 w. n E. fine - frost
24 w. E. fine frost.
25 w. E. fine - frost. Ash Wednesday - Mrs L & A Wilkinson
26 w. E. fine frost very cold.
27 w. n w. - fine - mild. - Received £10 from Mrs Kirkley.
28 w. n w. - fine & mild.
29 S w. n. fine - Congregation 26

March.

1 w. n. fine - mild
2 w. n. - fine - frost.
3 w. n E. fine - S E. frost.
4 w. S E. fine - very cold.
5 w. S. fine but cold.
6 w. S E. lovely warm day.
7 S w. S. beautiful bright day - Congregation - 38.
8 w. S. very fine.
9 w. S E. very fine. Out on Helvellyn with Crosher's dogs.
10 w. S E. fine - frost continues - n & n w.
11 w. w. fine - killed a Fox.
12 w. n w. glorious weather n w.
13 w. n E. fine - spring like
14 S w. n E. fine but cloudy - Congregation 27. Bazzy at Chapel for the first time.
15 w. n E. fine - cloudy.
16 w. n E. fine, cloudy. J. W. sowed the oats.
17 w. n E. - do
18 w. n E. fine & very mild, w. S E. bright evening.
19 w. S E. very fine - frosty. planted the field potatoes.

21 S w. S E. fine but very cold & windy. Congregation 25.
22 w. S. Mild Rain & warm - fine.
23 w. S w. delightful spring morng. finished field potatoes
24 w. E. fine but dark - very cold.
25 w. n E. fine but cold. Baptd. the baby at the Toll Gate.
26 w. n E. fine.
27 w. n E. fine - slight snow showers.
28 S w. S fine - Congregation 31.
29 w. S fine -
30 w. S E. Shower - windy - fine D. Thwaite sowing oats in the front field.
31 w. E - fine
Only once Rain in this month.

April.

1 w. n E very fine.
2 w. S E. very fine
3 w. S fine - at Keswick - (Paid 15/10 to John Graham
4 S. w. E. Snow showers - Cong. 15.
5 w. S E. very fine - pd. Jno. Birkett - 1.. 2.. 0
6 w. S E. very fine after frosty night.
7 w. E. fine - lovely weather
8 w. E fine -
9 w. n E fine - sup: fine.
10 w. n E. fine.
11 S w. n. fine very warm Easter day - Congregatn. 87 Communicts. 17.
12 w. E. S E. very fine.
13 w. S E. fine.
14 w. n E. S E. fine. very warm - School feast at Legburthwaite
15 w. S E fine - tea with old Mary
16 w. E. fine -
17 w. n E fine
18 S w. n E. Cloudy & cold - fine Cong. - 21.
19 w. S E. fine
20 w. S w. cloudy but fine - Evening warm
21 w. S w. fine - taking the annual
22 w. w. fair but cloudy & cold.
23 w. E. fine - Cuckoo heard by R. Thwaite
24 w. S E. fine but very windy.
25 S w. S E. fine - Congregation 27 - Saw a Swallow as coming from Chapel
26 w. n E. fine
27 w. S w. fine but cloudy

29 w, SW. [illegible] fine at night.
30 w, SW. Fair & mild.

May.

1 w, N. fine but cold
2 S w, NE. fine. Congregation - 26.
3 w, NE. drizzling rain - good rain.
4 w, NE. fine. went to Grasmere with Bez and Mama.
5 w, NE. fine but cloudy. Forwarded Mr Crewdsons letter to Revd. Sturmer.
6 w, NE. fine.
7 w, W. fine - cloudy.
8 w, W. fair but cloudy.
9 S w, SW. fine showers - Evening fine. W. Congregation 21.
10 w, SW. wet.
11 w, SW. very wet
12 w, W. Showers - fine - fished for the 1st time at Legber. caught two.
13 w, SW. mild showers.
14 w, NW. cold rain - fine
15 w, SW. fine
16 S w, SW. very wet - fine Evening. Congregation 14 -
17 w, SW. fine - went to Newlands.
18 w, NE. fine - cold - rain - John Hinde taken ill.
19 w, NE. wet - cold.
20 w, SE. fine - Ascension day.
21 w, SE. fine
22 w, NE. fine
23 S w, SE. fine - Congregation 41.
24 w, NE. fine - went to West Head to Tea.
25 w, NE. fine.
26 w, NE. fine - cold.
27 w, NE. fine but cloudy.
28 w, NE. fine. Confirmation at Keswick; on Helvellyn in the Evening.
29 w, NE. fine Whitsaturday.
30 S w, NE. fine. Congregation 21. Comm. 12. N.W.
31 w, NW. fine. very ill. { Heavy hail with Thunder all the fells white.

June.

1 w, N. fine
2 w, SW. Showers - heavy rain at night.
3 w, SW. showers.
4 w, SW. fine
5 w, SW. fine but dark.
6 S w, [illegible]
w, S. fine
7 E. fine but cloudy. went to Wigton
8 E. Showers. Visitation at Wigton.
9 NE. fine
10 w, N. fair but cloudy & cold.
11
12 w, SW. Showers - Evening fine - very mild.
13 S w, SW. fine - warm - Morning Congregation 33. Col: Sund. { Congregat: afternoon
14 w, W. Showers, but mild. Total - 80.
15 w, W. Showers, & mild.
16 w, W. wet
17 w, SW. fine [illegible] Thunder - rain
18 w, SW. fair but cloudy - Thunder
19 w, S. fine
20 S w, S. fine [illegible] Congregation - 36
21 w, S. fine
22 w, S. very wet - John Gillbanks washed Sheep
23 w, S. Showers - D. Thwaite washed his sheep.
24 w, W. fair - Cuckoo gone - last heard on Sunday the 20th.
25 w, SW. fine - but cloudy.
26 w, SW. wet - Evening fine.
27 S w, S. wet Congregation 24 - Collection for Churches 12/4 at Chapel.
28 w, W. wet - fine afterwards
29 w, SW. showers.
30 w, W. showers - fine. Jane Atkinson taken ill.
A fine vegetating month.

July.

1 w, W. fine - but cloudy. Mrs W. Cal. her Lodge.
2 w, W. [illegible] Showers - fine.
3 w, W. fine - at Keswick remitted 15/ to the Society for Churches.
4 S w, S. fine - Congregation 32.
5 w, S. fine, went to Helvellyn with Adam Wilkinson
6 w, S. slight heat shower - fine. Thunder Storm. (JW. began to mow
7 w, S. fine.
8 w, S. fine - very hot weather.
9 w, S. fine -
10 w, NW. fine - hot -
11 S w, SW. fine - Congregation 33.

12 w, SW. very fine - Geo Wilson's clipping.
13 w, SW Summer weather - Bolehead clipping. Thunder
14 w, SW - fine. — Thundery night.
15 w, W - misty & damp - T. Weightman's clipping. fine.
16 w, E - fine -
17 w, S - Rain - fair - fine
18 S w, S - fine — Congregation 36.
19 w, SW, very showery - fine - went to Penrith election.
20 w, SW - wet.
21 w, W - Shower - very fine - carried hay.
22 w, W Showery - fine - hot.
23 w, NE very fine.
24 w, SW - fine. First rate hay weather.
25 S w, S - fine but cloudy & hot. Congregation 33.
26 w, NE very wet - fine
27 w, E very fine.
28 w, E very fine. fine hay weather.
29 w, E - fine — Sharp shower - None in Wythburn.
30 w, E. fine — shower and "Pan cakes."
31 w, SW - fine. finished Hay.

Splendid month.

August -

1 S w, W - showers Congregation - 28.
2 w, W - fine but cloudy Revd. D. Coleridge at Arinbotts.
3 w, SW, very wet - W, fine.
4 w, W, fine
5 w, SW - wet - Showery.
6 w, SW - wet - showers
7 w, S - wet - showers -
8 S w, S - showers - fine - Congregation - 35.
9 w, SW - fine.
10 w, W, morning fine - showers.
11 w, E. morning fine - wet.
12 w, NE. very wet - NW - showers.
13 w, NW. very fine.
14 w, SW - very fine.
15 S w, NE - very fine - Congregation 39.
16 w, S. showers - wet - J. W. began to reap.
17 w, S - wet - wet -
18 w, W, fair - but doubtful.
19 w, E - fine
20 w, NW, fine
21 w, E - fine
22 S w, E - fine - very warm. Congregation 35.
23 w, W, fine - SW, slight shower.
24 w, W, fine - Baby born. — Ellen born
25 w, NW - fine - N - very fine.
26 w, W, fine.

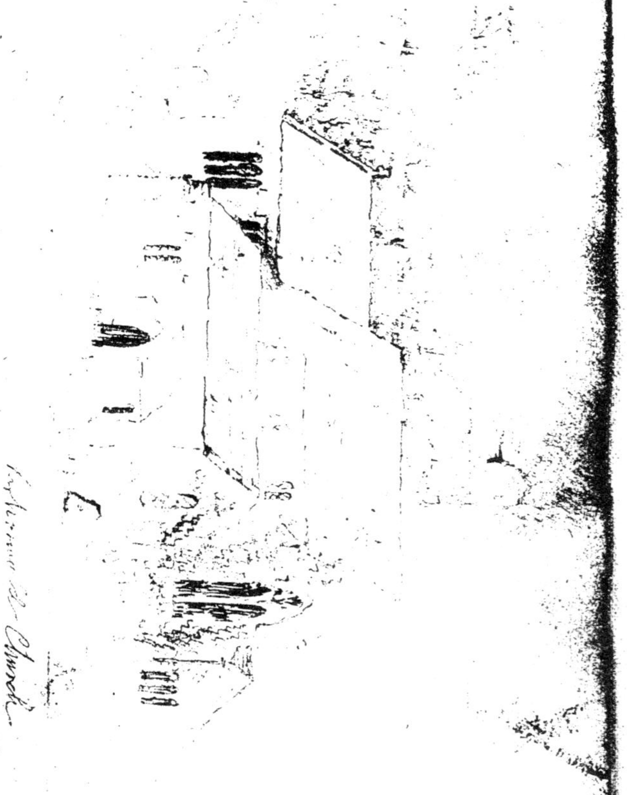

Kirkoswald Church
(Uncle Jerry.)

28 w. SW's fine. J. Wilkey [illegible] his grass & finished.
29 S w. SW. fine. Congregation 26.
30 w. SW. Showers & very wet night.
31. w. W. fine. –

Septumber.

1 w. SW. wet.
2 w. W. fine. Threlkeld fair.
3 w. S. fine.
4 w. S. fine
5 S w. SE. fine. Congregation 35.
6 w. S. wet.
7 w. SE. fine – hunting with Sir H. Vane's Hounds.
8 w. E. fine.
9 w. NE. fine
10 w. NE. fine.
11 w. NW. fine.
12 S w. N. fine. Congregation 25.
13 w. NW. fine
14 + w. NW. fine. Dr. Wilkinson left with his wife for Australia.
15 w. N. fine.
16 w. NE. fine.
17 w. NW. fine.
18 w. W. fine.
19 S w. NE. fine. Congregation 31. Ellen Christian Eddon
20 w. S. misty & showery.
21 w. NE. showers. fine. Rd. Forrest left for Australia
22 w. S. showery
23 w. W. fine. Sarah Gilbanks married by me at Grasmere
24 w. W. fine.
25 w. W. fine morning. Croster in Wythburn.
26 S w. NW. fine. Congregation 35.
27 w. E. wet. cold.
28 w. NE. wet – very wet & cold.
29 w. NE. wet.
30 w. NE. wet – mizzling.
31 w.

October. Mr. Martineau left Dalehead Hall.
1 w. W. showers.
2 w. W. fine.
3 S w. W. fine. Congregation 14. Communicants 9.
4 w. S. Morning fine. Evening very wet.
5 w. SW. wet. very wet
6 w. NW. fine.
7 w. NW. fine
8 w. N. fine but very cold. Trespatta [illegible].

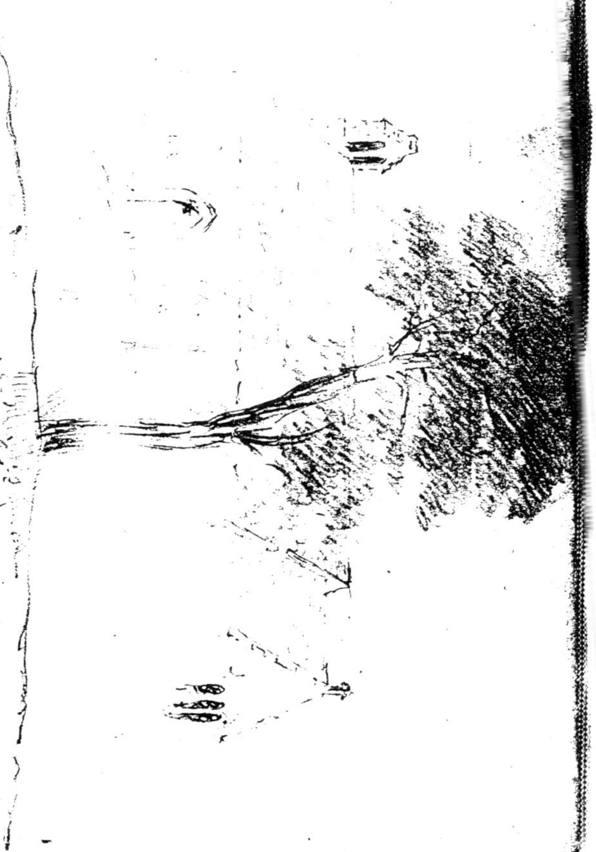

Legberthwaite Church.

9 w, N - fine - huul at Fornside
10 ✓ w, N - fine - Congregation - 34
11 w, N - fine
12 w, NW - fine - The last of the Martineaus left.
13 w, NW. fine - Sow littered 10 pigs.. Dalehead.
14 w, W - fine. -
15 w, S - fine but cold.
16 w, SE - fine - cold.
17 ✓ w, NE - fine - cold - Congregation 33
18 w, NW, fine, frosty -
19 w, NW, fine - went to Braithwaite to see Revd. Bird. -
20 w, W - fine.
21 w, W - Misty - Rain - fine.
22 w, SW - Misty & showers.
23 w, W, fine.
24 ✓ w, SW - Showers - Congregation 10 Mr. John Wilson arrived.
25 w, W - fine
26 w, NE - fine
27 w, NE - Showers
28 w, NE - fine but cold.
29 w, SW, wet.
30 w, SW - Showery John Rogers died.
31 ✓ w, SW - fine - Congregation - 15. -

November

1 w, W, very wet.
2 w, SW - fine - buried poor John Rogers at (Mattendale
3 w, SW - fine
4 w, SW - wet -
5 w, SW, very wet.
6 w, S - wet.
7 ✓ w, S - a deluge cd. not go to Wythburn. -
8 w, S. very wet & stormy.
9 w, SW - fine -
10 w, NW, fine.
11 w, S. very wet - Snow on the fells!!
12 w, E. very fine, very cold and wintery. Mrs. W. off for Cockermouth.
13 w, E. Rain & Snow.
14 ✓ w, SE - very stormy. Congregation 7.
15 w, S - fine.
16 w, SW fine.
17 w, S - Showery.
18 w, SW - fair
19 w, SW - Showers.
20 w, fair.
21 ✓ w, S - fair - Congregation 33.
22 w, NE. fair but misty
23 w, SW - fair
24 w, SW - fair
25 w, SW - fair but dark & cold.
26 w, SW - very stormy
27 w, W - fine.
28 ✓ w, S - hail showers - Congregn. 15. - Snow at night.
29 w, N. fine with frost & snow.
30 w, NE - hard frost.

December

1 w, W - wet morning - fine - Ball at Threlkeld.
2 w, NW - fine -
3 w, NW - fine. ——— 2nd Ball.
4 w, SW - very wet.
5 ✓ w, SW - Rain ——— Congregation 12.
6 w, W - Showers ——— fine
7 w, SW - fine. -
8 w, SW - wet -
9 w, NW - fine — John Birkbeck & his wife dined with us.
10 w, SW - wet -
11 w, SW - terrific storm of rain & wind.
12 ✓ w, S - a flood - violet Chapel - highest flood for 21 years.
13 w, NW - a lovely day.
14 w, S - wet -
15 w, S - wet -
16 w, SW - Showers.
17 w, S - very wet - NE -
18 w, NE - fine - very wet.
19 ✓ w, S - very wet - Congregation 4!!!
20 w, NW fine wet. Lord Derby Whispered ... for it.
21 w, NW - fine.
22 w, SW. fine -
23 w, S - fine - wet -
24 w, S - fine.
25 w, S - Xmas day - Terrific storm of wind - bridge blown away at Armboth.
26 ✓ w, S. fine - Congregatn. 10. 8 communicants. Congregatn. - 11.
27 w, S. terrific storm - fearful.
28 w, W fine.
29 w, SW very stormy.
30 w, S - wet.
31 w, S - another Rough day.

▽ Where the Armboth houses used to be from Dalehead side. △ Site of Hamlet of Armboth. ▽ Ruins of West Head. △ Dalehead Hall

Verses on pages with crudely drawn dogs and a cat, some scribble over what looks like a parson in frock coat and top hat Going to Staney.

Parson Lawson went fishing with Harry Pratt, a labourer in his late fifties who lodged at Fisher Place.

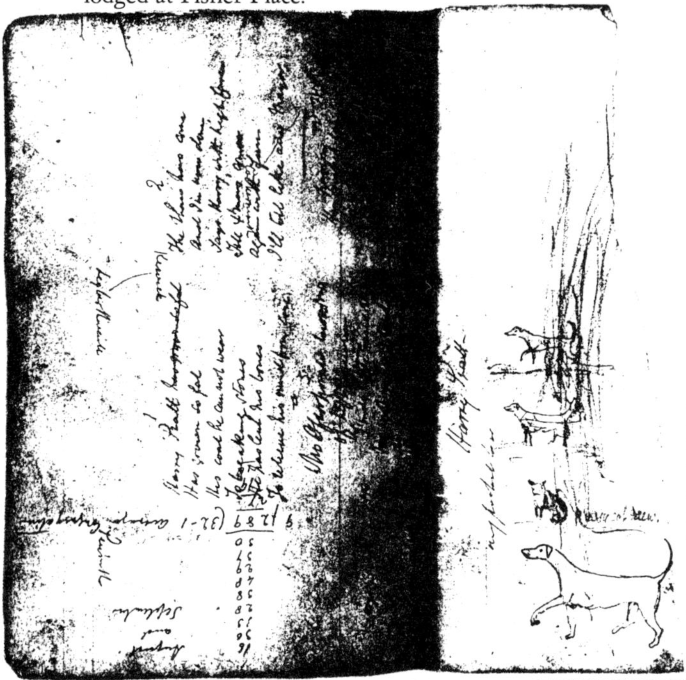

Harry Pratt
Has grown so fat
His coat he can not wear
To breaking stones
He has lent his bones
To relieve his mind from ca

The thaw has come
And I'm now done
Says Harry with high fare
Till Xmas comes
Again with fun
I'll toil like any Mayor

Who of corporate town
Of high renown
Finds little ease & rest
For with council feuds
And ------? broods
His mind is sorely pressed
His person pocket too,
pro bono pub
Has been with many a sub
Of angry d-------
(unfinished)

Sketches from the notebook.

Self portrait, or a parishioner?

As he might look in old age?

ALL SORTS AND CONDITIONS OF MEN

From April 1849 - December 1852 the primary purpose of Rev. Lawson's diary was to record his observations of the weather. Never for one day does he fail to do this but he seems so interested in all around him that other material has to be put down. An autobiography was not his intention but those few extra words manage to give an impression of a gregarious, humorous and vigorous man.

In these three years he does not even leave Cumbria but the people around him, family, friends, neighbours, congregations, celebrities and visitors are a kaleidoscope of interest. To investigate them all would be time-consuming, tedious and in many cases impossible. I have selected some diary entries concerning people and places and using researched material along with some guesswork have tried to tell more of the pattern of life revolving around the Parson of Wythburn almost a century and a half ago.

Although the mountain mists may clear to reveal a little detail in a valley below it is just as well to know in general, whereabouts one is. So, it is worthwhile to place the events in the Wythburn diary years within the context of the world outside.

Queen Victoria was in the twelfth year of her reign in 1849 and as Parson Lawson came home to Cumberland opened her third Parliament. In her speech from the throne, she expressed hopes for a suspension of arms amongst the contending parties of North and South Europe, mentioned that British and French admirals had intervened in Sicily to stop bloodshed and regretted a rebellion in the Punjab. The condition of manufacturing districts was encouraging and Her Majesty's Government would suggest the repeal of Navigation laws which hindered commerce. They would also seek the continuance of powers to deal with insurrection in Ireland and institute an enquiry into laws for the relief of the poor. Lord John Russell was the mildly reformist Prime Minister.

The Corn Laws had been repealed in 1846, allowing the import of cheaper grain; hours of work in factories had been limited by the Ten Hours Bill of 1847 and England was growing in wealth and power. The Great Exhibition of 1851 was set to demonstrate that prosperity to the rest of the world.

Only rarely does Rev. Lawson record national or international events:- December 20th 1852 'Lord Derby resigned - sorry for it.' Edward Stanley, fourteenth Earl of Derby succeeded Lord John Russell as Prime Minister. On July 19th 1852 there was a General Election and Parson Lawson went to Penrith for the election. C. W. G. Howard and William Marshall were the M.P.s elected for Cumberland East. Lord Derby's government was succeeded by a coalition cabinet led by Lord Aberdeen. What the Parson thought of that we do not know.

Earlier in 1852 he wrote 'considerable apprehensions of invasion by the French.' Prince Louis Napoleon, late president of France was now its emperor. The defeat of Waterloo rankled in French feeling and it was thought that the new emperor would be compelled to signalise his reign by an attempt to avenge it.

Within Britain 'Railway Mania' was spreading across the country. The Lancaster to Carlisle Railway opened in 1846, the nearest station to Wythburn being at Penrith and Windermere had its railhead by 1847. In January 1850 when Sir Henry Vane of Armathwaite came of age there was a great Gala Day on Bassenthwaite lake which had been covered with ice for a fortnight. The Cumberland Pacquet reported that merry makers played shinny and bandy, skating at 'Railway Speed.'

Old House in City, Wythburn.

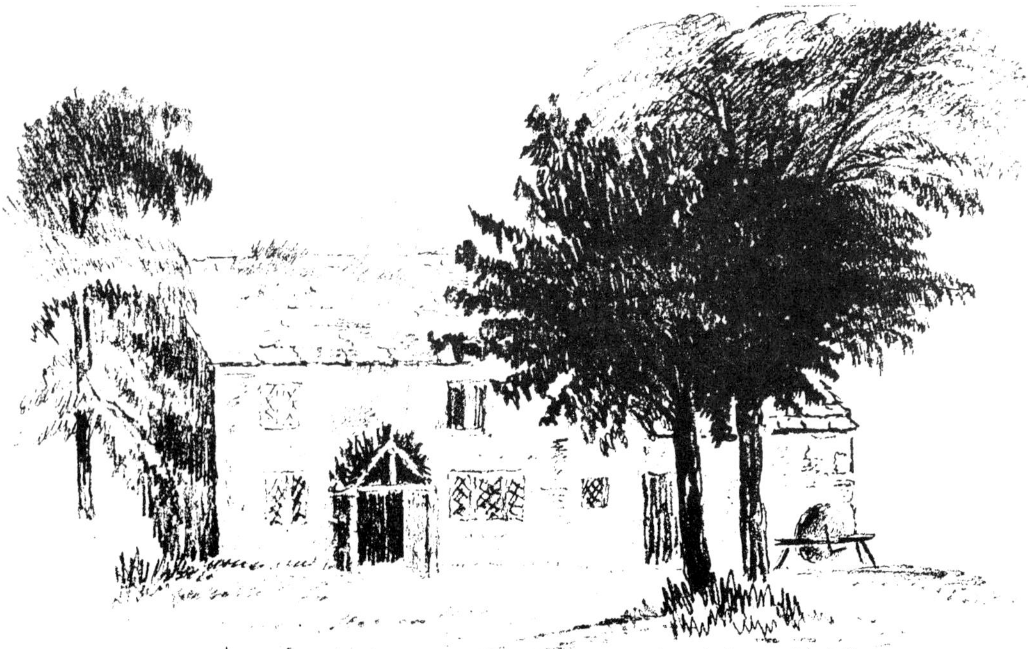

Lydy Hinde's house, Wythburn.

At Bank - overgrown, foundations still visible.

On the highways and byways, however the speed of a galloping horse was the fastest that anyone could travel. The coaches were fighting to compete with the new iron horses.

Cumberland Pacquet. August 20th 1850:-

> 'The coach fare between Cockermouth and Keswick is at the moment sufficiently low, we should imagine, to meet even the views of the most rabid free trader, and to fully come up to what in all matters is now considered the one thing needful - cheap, cheap, cheap. The distance is thirteen miles, the coaches new, drawn by four first rate horses and the fare only one shilling. This in point of cheapness beats even third class railway travelling.'

Only occasionally did this equine efficiency falter. Parson Lawson noted 20th Aug. 1849, 'coach broke down' and another time 'morning mail never arrived before six at night'. This would not please him as he carried on considerable correspondence with clerical friends, Rev. Sturmer, Rev. Whitby and Rev. Hartswell as well as Mr. Crewdson, Mr. Hooke, Bill Baker and others. He may have written to the papers as well, as in later years, he did when wished to protest against the Manchester Waterworks proposals. His opinions were printed in the correspondence column of the Westmorland Gazette which was likely to have been taken regularly as his source of local and general news.

Exploring the area on foot, Parson Lawson naturally shared his discoveries with his wife:- 24th May 1849 'Took my wife and Bazzy to the top of Great Howe'. From the Kings Head at Thirlspot it is a short, exhilarating but easy climb and seems to have been a favourite place of his. He made sketches of the Fisher Houses, Whiteside Fells and Helvellyn from the Howe. Mrs. L- was also taken to Raven Crag and with Bazzy to see the Waterfalls at Fisher Place. She must have found the crags, waterfalls and fells very different from the open landscape of her native county Leicestershire, especially when on 14th June 1849, her husband 'took my wife on Helvellyn, started at 12½, returned at six, a fine view of the Solway Firth & Morecambe Bay.'

Parson Lawson was certainly full of energy as details for four days in June 1849 demonstrate:-

'June 5th Went to Wigton
June 6th Slept at Scale Hill.
June 7th Walked to Keswick.
June 8th Climbed Helvellyn with Aylemore and Lloyd.' (Visitors?)

Scale Hill was an inn between Loweswater and Buttermere and about nine miles walking distance from Keswick.

One time he 'repaired the man (cairn) on Fisher Crag with Dodson and Hardisty' and another time 'went to Honister Crag with Dodson'. According to the 1851 Census, Mr. Hardisty was a lodger at Armboth. He is described as an Annuitant aged 45 and born at Keswick. He was near to the Parson in age and was a fishing companion as was Mr. Dodson who sometimes stayed at the Kings Head and sometimes at Armboth. There are notes of his arrivals and departures in winter and summer.

As would be expected Parson Lawson went frequently to Keswick, sometimes with his wife and child. He would have parochial business there and on 12-13th March 1851 brackets two days with 'at Keswick - Vic-' as if he had duties there. Reverend John Lynn was the Vicar of Crosthwaite but it is known that he was absent for long periods and left the churches in the care of his curates. While in Keswick Parson Lawson may have read in the new library, founded by the Rev.

Town Head, Grasmere.

Frederick Myers, the first incumbent of St. John's, Keswick. It was built opposite the school and his church. The delightful group of buildings remain, only a little altered and still well used. Although the library is no longer used for that purpose the remnants of the original book stock can be seen in the newer County Library in north Keswick.

Parson Lawson also visited Grasmere, Penrith and Carlisle occasionally but when there was time for a short holiday he, and presumably his family, went to Lazonby, the lovely village in the red sandstone valley of the River Eden. Nearby, at Kirkoswald was the church where Uncle George, Gerard George Lawson had been Vicar since 1832. A sketch was made in the little notebook of 'Uncle George's church' and of the old church at Lazonby, now completely rebuilt. Kirkoswald's ancient church has changed little. Once a collegiate church with a detached bell tower built in the time of Henry the Eighth, the porch is reached by walking through a green tunnel made by an avenue of fragrant lime trees. Parson Lawson must have trodden the stone flagged path of the 'priests walk' to enter the church of St. Oswald and view the fresh stained glass put into the chancel's two windows in 1846. Was he, perhaps, gratified to see the 'two arms embowed vested Erminois cuffed Sable holding a sun in his splendour', the crest of the Lawsons of Isel, amongst the other heraldic devices. The windows commemorate the Dacre and Musgrave families into which Lawsons had married. It is doubtful whether he could claim any connection with the County family but Lawsons elsewhere have used the distinctive crest and he would certainly recognise it.

Contacts were made in the Eden Valley and years later one of Rev. Lawson's daughters Henrietta Ada, baptised in 1855 was to settle there. She married in 1882, John Watson Nelson, a widower of Eden Bank, Langwathby.

On June 24th 1849, while at Lazonby, Parson Lawson wrote 'missed my brother as usual.' Perhaps the brother had been there some other time or perhaps he had called at Wythburn but the Parson did not miss seeing his sister, Miss Lawson. She came to stay for four days in the months of July 1849 and 1850. Tamar Ann Lawson was a spinster aged about fifty in 1849. The 1841 Census yields the information that she was a governess at the home of her father, Heversham Vicarage. There were fifteen girls in her care as well as her aged father. She managed with the help of only two indoor servants.

Miss Ada Hallam wrote to me 'Aunt Tamar Ann was the bane of my mother's existence. She kicked up rows, every time she came to stay at Wythburn.' Miss Hallam's mother, Fanny, Parson Lawson's youngest daughter passed on these memories of later years of course but there is no hint that the Parson was pleased to see his sister in 1849 and 1850.

All the families living in the Thirlmere valley would know The Parson of Wythburn and some of them became friends and companions as well as parishioners. Jane Westray of the Kings Head was the Lawson's landlady and the first source of information for the new curate. She would seem to have been a personality of some account, indeed Parson Lawson mentions her rather more in three years than he does his wife. Soon after arrival he mentions her anxiety about a lame horse. Since she was a lady who liked to get about this must have been serious, comparable with the breakdown of a little runabout car in contemporary terms. There were grounds for worry. The Parson notes that on 21st April 1849 the horse was worse and on 22nd it died!

Jane was not a native of Wythburn. She came from Embleton near Cockermouth, and was born there in 1793, the elder daughter of John and Elizabeth Rothery. They were of farming stock as was Jonathon Westray whom she married in 1815. Jane was twenty-two and Jonathon was forty. Was Jonathon a widower or a bachelor suddenly attracted to a young woman? The brief parish records do not indicate but maybe the fact that five months later on April 12th 1816, a son, Joseph was baptised suggests a possible reasons why Jane married, by license, a man eighteen years older than herself. They farmed at Beckbank in Embleton and there another son, John was born in 1818 and a daughter, Elizabeth in 1820.

By 1829 the family were in residence at Thirlspot. Jonathon Westray is listed in the Parson and White Directory of Cumberland and Westmorland as victualler at the Kings Head, Legberthwaite.

A few years later entries in the Embleton Parish registers chillingly record what must have been a traumatic period in Jane's life. In 1836 Jonathon died aged sixty-one: in 1837 Elizabeth died aged seventeen and in 1839 Jane's younger son died aged twenty-one.

They were not interred at Saint John's in the Vale, the usual graveyard for Legberthwaite at that time but three times in three years Jane must have made the journey back to Embleton to see them buried at home. All were laid to rest in unmarked graves.

The 1841 Census gives Jane Westray as the publican at the Kings Head with son Joseph, an agricultural labourer, plus a farm servant and a man servant. Evidently she had the strength of character to carry on and run a busy inn. Change was afoot, however, by October 1849 the Kings Head was let and in March 1850 after a sale at which there was a fight, the whole household removed to Armboth. Here there was less land for Joseph to farm and Jane Westray was released from the business of running an inn, although she still had some rooms which she let as lodgings.

Enjoying some freedom, on April 23rd 'Mrs. Westray went to Cockermouth for the Fair.' She went again in October and came back in November with the news of the burning of Cockermouth church.

The subsequent report in the Cumberland Pacquet reads:-

> 'On the morning of Friday 15th November 1850 the Church at Cockermouth was destroyed by fire. About half-past one on the morning Police Officer Chapman whilst passing over Cocker Bridge discovered sparks issuing from the church and he immediately called up several persons and an alarm was instantly spread throughout the town. In a short time an immense concourse of people had assembled around the conflagration.'

When just after Christmas Mrs. Westray set off for Cockermouth once more, Parson Lawson records, rather testily '4th time in 10 months' but back she came on 12th January 1851. On November 9th the same year he says simply that she 'Left home' and returned on 20th. As in the previous year December 30th was the day that Mrs. Westray 'went to Cockermouth' but the parson seems to be getting used to it as he does not mention her return and only one other record of these excursions is made on November 12 1852, 'Mrs. W. off for Cockermouth.'

For a number of years the Lawson Family and the Westrays lived under the same roof with the Lawson children and the grandchildren of Jane playing together in the meadows and becks and Parson Lawson interested in Joseph's farming progress. However, the third Lawson baby was born in 1855 at Wheyfold (Queyfold) a house near to the church at Wythburn. The Westrays must also have moved away from Armboth since the name disappears from local records and so came the parting of the ways.

To return to the days of the diary:- When the two families removed to Armboth the Hall had been to let for over a year. February 12th 1849 in the Cumberland Pacquet.

LAKE RESIDENCE TO LET
ARMBOTH HOUSE

> To let for Seven or more years. That delightful Country Residence, Armboth House, situate in the sweetest nook of one of the most Picturesque Vales of the Lake District, being near the foot of Thirlmere Lake and about six miles from Keswick, and near the coach road to Ambleside.
>
> The Mansion consists of Dining and Drawing rooms, Library, Servant Hall, Kitchen, Dairy etc. on the ground floor with Numerous rooms and comfortable attics above, along with Coach House, Stables and other requisites and with or without Thirty acres of land surrounding the Premises. All having been in the possession of the late W. Jackson Esq. till recently. Mr. Adam Wilkinson, on the place will show the premises.
>
> Mr. Dickinson of North Mosses, Cockermouth will furnish particulars and treat for the same as soon as an adequate offer in writing is made. Immediate possession may be had.

Otter Bield at Raven Crag.

House in Wythburn.

The advertisement then appeared weekly until the end of August. Perhaps it was because Armboth House had the reputation of being haunted. 'Lights are seen there at night, the people say; and the bells ring; and just as the bells are set off ringing, a large dog is seen swimming across the lake. The plates and dishes clatter; and the table is spread by unseen hands. That is the preparation for the ghostly wedding feast of a murdered bride, who comes up to keep her terrible nuptials. There is really something remarkable and like witchery about the house. On a bright moonlight night the spectator who looks towards it from a distance of two or three miles sees the light reflected from its windows into the lake, might easily be taken for an illumination of a great mansion. And this mansion seems to vanish as you approach - being no mansion but a small house lying in a nook, and overshadowed by a hill.'

So wrote Harriet Martineau in her 'Complete Guidebook to the Lakes', published first in 1855. It is possible that she was gathering the material for this when she stayed at Dalehead Hall in October 1852. Parson Lawson noted this down with underlining which seems to indicate that the entry does refer to the well known Victorian blue-stocking living at The Knoll in Ambleside. Certainly her brother and his family were friends of the Leathes of Dalehead. Norman Nicholson in the Lakers tells how she hired a wagonette and toured the district with six friends. On 12th October Parson Lawson notes "The last of the Martineaus left Dalehead.'

There are some vividly descriptive phrases from Harriet Martineau's Guide Book which tell us what the western shore of Thirlmere was like before the flooding. She passes by the few cottages called by the 'boastful name of the City of Wythburn' and then, following the rude road comes upon 'a grassy level under the Armboth Fells, within an amphitheatre of rocks.' The rocks are 'feathered with wood, except where a bold crag here, and cataract there, introduces a variety.'

She warns of the dangers of scrambling up the rocks to the top of the waterfalls at Lancey Gill (Launchey Gill) but says that the tourist who does so is rewarded with 'a view of King Helvellyn and the nobles of his court at Thirlmere.'

Safely down from the gill, past a clear pool where herons fish 'the track leads by the margin of the lake and through a shady lane and a farmyard to the bridge by which the lake is crossed'. It is still possible to discern the tumbled stones of the farm house, find broken household pots under mounds of earth and when the water is low, tread upon the cobbles of the yard of Yew How farm.

Harriet Martineau then crossed the bridge over the shallows to Dalehead Hall which also had its legends of murder and ghosts. Hall Caine used tales of the hauntings in his novel 'The Shadow of a Crime.'

None of this seems to have bothered Parson Lawson or Mrs. Westray who 'let her Lodgings' frequently. Like so many other myths and legends they are kept alive because the locals enjoy the telling of them and long may they continue.

While Armboth House was being advertised another companion of Parson Lawson was there to show the premises to would be tenants. In the Parson and White Directory of 1829 he is listed as a schoolmaster but in 1841 is, according to Census returns, manservant to Wilson Jackson. Adam Wilkinson is one of the few people that Parson Lawson refers to using a christian name only:- '24th April 1851, a beautiful day, the wind changing round from south to west and giving thunder, went to Raven Crag with Adam'. In July of that year Adam spent the night on Armboth fell, whether by design, to see the sunrise or by accident it would be interesting to know but the diarist is brief as he is also in August when he writes 'Adam started for London' on 22nd and on 30th 'Adam returned from London'. Did he visit the top attraction in the capital that year The Great Exhibition and bring reports back to Wythburn? The next summer they were together on Helvellyn again.

Adam, Dodson, Hardisty and Pratt were companions for outdoor pursuits but there were gentler social occasions of coming and going between the valley dwellings and a great deal of the taking of tea. 'tea at Dalehead' notes Parson Lawson on November 18th 1849. Farming at
Dalehead were the Thwaites, Daniel aged seventy-six and his son Reuben aged forty-six. The Lawsons reciprocated. 'Jan 8th 1850 D. Thwaite took tea with us' and in 1852 an indication that then, as now, the long dark northern winter nights were whiled away playing Bridge. 'Jan 14 Reuben and John A (Atkinson of the Kings head) played a rubber at A'th'.

Farmer Thomas Weightman and his wife Mary of Nether Place had, in 1851, three sons and two daughters living at home. Some of them came to Armboth House on January 7th 1852:- 'Thos Weightman & C. tea'd with us.' Mary Cole from Hollin Brow and Sarah Walker from the Cherry Tree came together for tea on September 9th 1851 but the most mentioned are the Gillbanks of West Head. August 13th 1850 'Went to West Head with Bazzy and Mama'; August 15th 1851 'Mr. and Mrs. Gillbanks visited us'; ten days later 'went to West Head to tea'; September 11th 'the girls from West Head tea'd with us' and in May of the next year 'went to West Head to tea'.

The farm house at West Head housed a large family. John and his wife, Mary were in their mid-fifties and had four sons and three daughters with ages ranging from twenty-seven to nine. There is no doubt that the two families became great friends and that the Gillbanks loved and supported the church at Wythburn. Parson Lawson officiated when twenty-six year old Sarah was married at Grasmere and when he made his will in 1882 it was witnessed by John Gillbanks Jnr. and Mary Gillbanks. At the time of the tea parties, James the youngest boy was only nine, however twelve years later he had erected the first gravestone in Wythburn churchyard.

Burials did not take place there until Wythburn became a separate parish in 1862. The first stone tells a poignant tale of the deaths, within days of each other, of the ten month old twins of a lead miner

> Jane and John the beloved twins of John and Isabella Arnison of Pinfold How, Wythburn who departed this life on the 17th and 30th March 1863 aged ten months.
>
> Erected by James Gillbanks of Wythburn in kind remembrance of the above twins being the first interred in this burial ground.

Why it was James who provided this memorial we do not know. Later he took over the farm at Stenkin while John Jnr. still farmed at West Head. At the present time a house at Steel End is known as West Head Farm while the West Head of Parson Lawson's day is a heap of untidy stones and only imagination can bring back the activity and the laughter of the young people who worked and played there. From the yard outside the front door, groups of walkers gaze across the valley to the only building visible, the white church beside which some of the Gillbanks rest.

It must have comforted the family that their good friend conducted the burial service for Margaret aged forty-seven in 1878 and her father John who was ninety when he died in 1883. Others, who moved away to Arnside have their memorials beside them, including James, who erected with such compassion the first stone and saw so much change before he died in 1914.

Taking tea, Parson Lawson mentioned often, dining only twice. Nov. 5th 1850 'Dined at Dalehead with the Suttons' probably visitors, and December 9th 1852 'John Banks and his wife dined with us.'

John Banks is mentioned in two other entries. On a cold but fine Ash Wednesday in 1851 he was the only person at chapel and he turned up again on Ascension Day. This time his name is underlined. Positive identification of John Banks is not possible as no one of that name appears in the 1851 Census or relevant Directories for Wythburn. In Keswick there were several families of Banks, including a pencil manufacturer.

A Mr. Bragg arrived early on June 17th 1849 and 'breakfasted with us'. Some weeks previously Parson Lawson had noted 'Bragg preached at St. John's, so it seems that he was one of the clerical gentlemen who found themselves welcome at Legberthwaite and Wythburn. 'Rev. Wilson called' on 13th November 1849. Edward Wilson was the perpetual curate of St. John's in the Vale but lived on Ambleside Road in Keswick. When he died aged seventy-two he had been incumbent at St. John's for forty-eight years and rests in the churchyard there with his father, also a clergyman and a native of Keskadale in Newlands.

Parson Lawson had only been at the Kings Head a matter of weeks when Mr. Bird called. This was not surprising as F. J. Carruthers tells in his book 'Around the Lakeland Hills' of Parson Bird of Braithwaite Lodge who was one of the gentlemen who took up coaching for coaching's sake. He was specially interested in a service through Keswick called 'The Cuckoo' and so great was his interest that he would ride alongside the coach for miles watching the horses at work and the coachman manipulating the ribbons. When the coachman of the Cuckoo met with an accident and broke a leg Parson Bird actually took over the driving for a time, giving his fees to the crippled coachman. Parson Bird, who was also Vicar of Ainstable in the Eden valley sounds like a man of action; a man who would find a kindred spirit in the energetic Parson Lawson. He went to Braithwaite to see Parson Bird on the 19th October 1852.

A clergyman with a more academic claim to fame appears on 2nd August 1852, 'Rev. D. Coleridge at Armboth' Derwent Coleridge, the second son of Samuel Taylor Coleridge would be well known in the district. He had recently published the poems and memoirs of his poet brother, Hartley who died in 1849 and was probably enjoying a vacation, being in 1852 the Principal of Saint Mark's College, Chelsea.

There are many notes confirming that the Parson was in the homes of his flock at times of birth, death, trouble and joy; naturally he became a trusted confidant. Three times he mentions calling on Nancy Dawson, a lady in her eighties living at Stennack and on one occasion writes, 'Old Nancy told me she had made her will'. He went to see Lyddy Hinde on the 15th September 1851. Lyddy was the fifty-five year old wife of James Hinde of Bank Farm and was the recipient of a much more disturbing call in later years when Sir John Harwood came with a packet of tea and prevailed upon the widowed Lyddy to persuade her son, George to sell the farm to the Manchester Waterworks Committee. Harwood promised her that if she did so she could remain there for the rest of her days which she did. Bank Farm was eventually demolished and George went to High Field Side at Keswick but was brought back to the place of his birth and buried at Wythburn when he died in 1898.

Social contacts also came from a little further afield:- June 10th 1850 'Miss Skelton and Mrs. Brougham came to see us'. On the first of the month Parson Lawson wrote 'Miss Skelton thrown out of a gig on Whinlatter' and two days later 'went to see Miss Skelton'. There was a previous entry on the 6th May 1849, simply 'Heard of Miss Skelton', so there may have been earlier acquaintance. The Skeltons were from Foulsyke, Loweswater. Miss Skelton and Mrs. Brougham were sisters, daughters of Joseph Skelton and might be described as minor gentry. When the 1851 Census was taken the house at Foulsyke was occupied by only Mrs. Brougham's children, James aged six and Mary Isabel with four servants and a governess. James Brougham became a Major and a J.P. and inherited the Loweswater estate.

One September day in 1849 Parson Lawson recognised a notable person in the district. 'Lord Langdale on Helvellyn' he writes. An honoured Westmorland man, Henry Bickersteth, Baron Langdale was born at Kirkby Lonsdale. He was called to the Bar in 1811, became Solicitor General and was Master of the Rolls for fifteen years. He took a peerage on condition that he might have entire political independence and devote himself to law reform. It was through his perseverance that government was persuaded to provide an adequate repository for national records. In 1850, he took over duties of Speaker of the House of Commons, during the illness of the Speaker, Lord Cottenham. He was offered the Chancellorship by Lord John Russell, but declined. He died in 1851 and the barony became extinct. Surprisingly, since they had spent their early years within ten miles of each other, Parson Lawson did not record his death.

There are few occasions when any dealings with trades people are specifically noted down. All of that must have been left to his wife or Mrs. Westray. However, on 3rd April 1852, Parson Lawson paid 15/10 to John Graham at Keswick and two days later 'pd Jno Birkett £1.2.0'. John Birkett, then over eighty was the cordwainer or shoemaker living at the City, so possibly Parson Lawson had purchased shoes or had boots repaired. A matter of interest is that when he came to Wythburn the very first entry that he made in the registers was the baptism of John Birkett's grandaughter, Mary, child of son George and his wife Mary. There was another John Birkett farming at the City, but payment to the shoemaker seems the most likely.

What a variety of human beings, noble and base, were in and around Legberthwaite and Wythburn in those four years of the mid nineteenth century. Family memories, say that later, the Rev. Lawson entertained Mathew Arnold and several Bishops, including William Temple who became Archbishop of Canterbury. Someone of the baser kind however, must have been responsible for the occasion in August 1950 when 'tollgate at Wythburn robbed, when John Hawkrigg lost his shirt and shoes-&c.'

With those neither noble nor base, Parson Lawson and his family had plenty of opportunity for fun and frolic. He records markets and fairs, a shepherd's feast, Legberthwaite school feast, Keswick sports and a Merry night. Each year there is a 'Xmas party at Trespath'; in 1852 it becomes a 'ball'. The Trespath Ball (Thirlspot) would be hosted by John Atkinson of the Kings Head and it is just possible that John Richardson and his wife, Grace formerly a Birkett of the City, were present. He was at that time a stonemason, working for his father and

John Crozier 1822 - 1903.

Thomas Stanger Leathes,
Lord of the Manor of Legberthwaite, died 1878.

George Leathes.
Sold the Manor to Manchester, 1879.

living at Piper Houses in Saint John's in the Vale. Six years later, this remarkable man was to become the schoolmaster at St. John's for almost the rest of his life. He also wrote poems and tales of the life around him in dialect, publishing 'Cummerland Talk' in 1871. Like the Parson, he enjoyed fishing the lake and his 'Thowts by Thirlmere' cannot be beaten for homespun philosophy but it is in his introduction to the book that he gives an incomparable picture of the changes that must have been going on during Parson Lawson's ministry.

'During the last sixty or seventy years there has been a complete transformation among the rural population of Cumberland, in their diet, dress and manners. Instead of the oatmeal porridge, oatmeal bread, salt beef and home-brewed ale, which were then almost their sole living; wheat bread, tea, coffee, sugar and other articles which were then thought great luxuries may now be found in the poorest cottage. Instead of the coarse Skiddaw-grey coats and the linsey- woolsey gowns and petticoats which were then universally worn by young and old; the finest broadcloths, merinos, alpacas and even silks are common in every dwelling. Instead of the roistering merry-nights, weddings, bridewains and other gatherings described by Anderson and Stagg, the annual gatherings are designated 'balls' and are generally as well conducted, and as free from anything objectionable, as the balls and assemblies among the higher classes.'

The scope and speed of transformation in rural Cumberland has continued with increasing momentum to the present day. But, go to the gathering in a Threlkeld Inn after a run with the Blencathra pack or attend the Hunt Ball and you will see the indigenous people, the same easy mix of social classes - and even hear the songs that rang out at the feasts of Parson Lawson and his friends.

There was a rough and stormy end to 1852 and with ten more days of weather observations for January of the next year, a few verses, a paragraph and drawings, the little brown book is finished. The short span of the time of the diary becomes part of the passage of the centuries. The valleys lit by a stray beam of light are part of the whole landscape as the sun burns off the mist. The Vale of Thirlmere that in 1851 sustained the lives of about two hundred souls has to give of its resources for the needs of millions.

DUNMAIL IN SEPULCRA TREMENS

The baby, Mary Jane Richardson, baptised at the Tollgate by Parson Lawson on 25th March 1852, would barely have reached marriageable age before the inhabitants of Wythburn would be aware that their homes and the fields and fells around were under scrutiny.

All the great cities of Britain, expanding and prospering needed a good water supply to serve the factories and ensure that the growing populations were able to wash themselves and their clothes. The zealous city councils planned on a grandiose scale to house and educate the workers necessary to the building of an industrial nation. They saw a vision of a British Empire dominating the world and bringing considerable profits in the process. Medical opinion insisted that a pure water supply was essential and the city fathers set out to obtain it for Birmingham, Liverpool and Manchester. They lifted up their eyes to the hills of the west and the north.

Alderman Grave of Manchester, who was born at Cockermouth and had a house at Portinscale knew the Lake District well. He brought other members of the Waterworks Committee to the area to consider suitable sites. 'The History and Description of the Thirlmere Water Scheme' written by Sir John James Harwood (Knight) published in 1895, tells the full story of the acquisition, the construction and engineering works through to the opening of the dam. The book is now out of print and difficult to obtain but I would recommend Molly Lefebure's excellent chapter entitled 'The Cherry Orchard of Armboth' in her book 'Cumberland Heritage', Gollancz 1970 to anyone wishing to understand the conflicts of opinion and the inevitability of the outcome. The story that I have to tell is of the involvement of Parson Lawson and the people that he knew.

Having decided on Thirlmere as the site for a reservoir the Manchester Waterworks Committee proposed purchasing 11,000 acres of land. Surveys had to be made and it was realised that the land would go up in value when the plans became public knowledge. With experience gained elsewhere, it was also decided that the farms around the lake must be bought to avoid costs and liability for cattle straying and drowning in water courses. It seems that the Committee thought that this could be quietly accomplished but they did not consider the gossip that would be exchanged at the Kings Head and the Nags Head or mulled over at clippings and feasts. The residents, while not believing that the rumours they heard were even possible, would nevertheless be on their guard.

Three Keswick men were hired to obtain the information that the Committee wanted. Mr. David Pape was a cattle dealer in the neighbourhood and had a good idea of the value of land; Mr. Thomas Dixon Lancaster, a builder was to value the buildings and Mr. Jenkinson was supposed to be collecting material to write a guidebook. Were the locals likely to be so easily fooled?

Dalehead Hall, it was thought would make an excellent headquarters and country house for the Aldermen, their managers, designers and architects. Thomas Stanger Leathes, Lord of the Manor of Legberthwaite refused his permission for Alderman Grave and Alderman Harwood to look over the place. In spite of this the dignitaries were determined to find out what they could. Choosing a wet and miserable day, the Aldermen crept on their hands and knees past the Hall. Mrs. Thwaite came out from Dalehead Farmhouse and ordered them off. Her husband's family had spent all of their lives in the service of the Leathes family. Alderman Harwood and his companion, he recalls were afterwards laid up with colds. perhaps it served them right.

In 1876, Manchester City Council confirmed a resolution to buy the required land. The following year letters began to appear in local and national newspapers, evaluating, objecting to and sometimes applauding the scheme. Articles were written and one of these prompted Parson Lawson to write to the Westmorland Gazette of February 17th 1877:-

> Sir, -- In the Manchester Courier of February 6th there is an article entitled "Manchester Water Supply and Thirlmere Scheme", in which it is said that the lake is called "Leatheswater from its having belonged to Mr. T. S. Leathes of Dalehead House". Why did the writer of the paragraph use the words "having belonged to Mr. T. S. Leathes?" Why refer to the dead, and why not say "Belongs to Mr. George Leathes", the present owner of the lake, and who, we all here hope, may long remain so. Leatheswater did not obtain its name from the late Mr. T. S. Leathes. The lake enjoyed the name for a long period before the late Mr. Leathes took the possession or ownership of it.
>
> That the present owner may have made some arrangement to part with

some of his shore land to forward the scheme of the Manchester Waterworks I can believe, because the extension of his lake would in fact be the curtailment of the manor of Wythburn. So it appears to my judgement, inasmuch as, hitherto, to whatever height Leatheswater rises, so far on its shore the Lord of Dalehead claims the land for his fishing purposes. Therefore extend Thirlmere from Raven Crag in the north end of the lake up to Steel-end in the south and the addition to Mr. Geo. Leathes's manorial authority is pretty considerably to the disadvantage of the lord of the manor of Wythburn.

But this view only interests great men. We smaller ones have an interest in Wythburn which perhaps as acutely affects us. It is the place of our birth, or it has become endeared to us from long residence. Such being the case, it need be no surprise that (if non- resident owners are indifferent to the project of submerging our valley) they who are resident oppose it; and such is the case. Opposed this project is, and will be, which requires a whole parish to be submerged and its inhabitants driven to seek their home elsewhere. We cannot be expected resignedly to submit, nor to await our fate with complacency.-- Yours truly, B. R. Lawson.

The next week there was a reply from an anonymous person who headed his letter with the very apt words "Dunmail in Sepulcra Tremens". His theme was that the Lordships of manorial areas depended on Ancient Royal Grants and that the Leathes family could not benefit from the expansion of the lake. Manorial boundaries 'could not expand or vary with newborn exploits of modern engineering' Dunmail continued:- ' "primeval Thirlmere" will really be no more and ancestral "Leatheswater" a thing of the past and instead "The Great Manchester Reservoir" will be the grand new prose for the poetry of ages.' He concludes:- 'When, too, he deplored the watery destruction of a whole parish, its kirk, God's acres and homesteads did he really not remember that by this Cottonopolis will be able to wash her dirty linen in the tears of the drowned out "oldest inhabitants" and to energise her factory engines, and brew her "Souchong" with the dews and cataracts of mighty Helvellyn.
Yours &c.'

On March 3rd Parson Lawson's response was published. He begins:- 'I regret that in my last letter I should have written anything offensive to King Dunmail. I can assure the Royal Spirit that I never thought that the antiquity of the Leathes family was a question before the public, or needed to be asserted in these days, or I might more fully have entered into it.'

He went on to say that he regretted that King Dunmail should be annoyed, but rejoiced that he should return to the world from which he had so long retired in order to vindicate claims which the Leathes family might have on him and ends 'doubtless the King was billeted on the Leathes family at Dalehead and supped and enjoyed himself with them on the evening before the day of the fight which ended so fatally. This my first "fratch" with royalty must be may last. In the hope that we may near no more moans from the cairn, I remain.

Yours truly, B. R. Lawson. Feb 28 1877'

'Dunmail' did have some other correspondence but not with Parson Lawson. Loch Katrine had already been utilised as a water supply and he was involved in a series of letters debating whether or not the Scottish loch had been spoiled and if so whether the same situation would arise at Thirlmere. Some of these letters came from Mr. Robert Crewdson of Rydal Mount, who when the Westmorland

Gazette reported on July 14th 1877 that there had been a unanimous vote by the Corporation of Manchester to carry out the Thirlmere Water Scheme, wrote again pointing out that the Water Board had in mind the selling of water and that the public health was a lesser consideration. He then put on record the same hope that has been the last cry of all defeated protesters to so many enterprises supposed to be for the public good.' If it is to go ahead we must see that the lines which Nature has laid down are not too readily overstepped.'

Dunmail, the last King of Strathclyde and Cumbria lost his battle in 945 A.D. with the English Edmund. The large heap of stones on the Raise at approximately the old Westmorland, Cumberland border, commemorates Dunmail's stand, not his burial place. Likewise the inhabitants of Wythburn did not submit to Manchester without a fight. Parson Lawson mentioned in his letter to the Westmorland Gazette that Mr. George Leathes was the owner of the estate which his family had held since 1577. Thomas Stanger Leathes, who had refused to sell was dead and George, son and heir was in Australia. His only interest in the estate was the income which it provided but other members of the family kept up the opposition for some time. Without success, for the Corporation of Manchester became owners of the Hall and lands in 1879.

Sir Harry Vane, of Hutton Hall agreed to part with his land, provided that he kept the rights of shooting and sporting over Armboth Fell for the rest of his life.

The most troublesome landowner, however proved to be the representative of the Jackson family of Armboth, Mary, Countess Ossalinsky. The story of her fight against the authorities has captured the public imagination, has been well documented and often recounted. The local girl of yeoman stock who married a 'Russian or Polish Count' and held the City of Manchester Corporation to ransom became almost a fairytale heroine.

As usual, things are not always as they seem.

The Jacksons were dalesmen of long standing but Wilson Jackson, Mary's grandfather seems to have been the last to make Armboth House his permanent home. His son, Edward Washington Jackson, an attorney died in 1825, leaving Mary his only surviving child to inherit the estate. At eighteen she married the so called Count Ossalinsky and went to live at Chestnut Hill House in Keswick. Her only son, Vladimir Boris and a daughter who died in infancy were born there. The marriage did not last long. Ossalinsky is reputed to have been a scoundrel and there is some doubt as to whether he was the 'Count' that he claimed to be. In 1843 another birth was registered at Wythburn, Sep. 24th. 'Nathalie d. of -- & Mary Ossalinsky. Armboth House'. In the column for father's trade or profession, Count Ossalinsky is written but by then he is believed to have gone abroad, where he died in 1859.

When Parson Lawson came to Wythburn, Wilson Jackson and his wife were both dead and it is unlikely that Mary and the children were often at Armboth. Mary continued to use the title of 'Countess' and it is probably that the very sound of the name 'Countess Ossalinsky' was helpful in impressing the Manchester officials. The full story of her battle, not so much to retain the land as to receive a larger settlement than the Corporation's original valuation of £20-25,000, is told in Alderman Harwood's book.

Manchester Corporation finally paid out £77,000 excluding the value of the sheep, but the Countess had really worried the Aldermen and the Waterworks Committee. Harwood recommended that a Bill should be put to Parliament for

Local Government Powers to appoint an arbitrator in future cases. The Lands Clauses Act of 1883 empowered the Board of Trade to appoint an umpire when similar situations arose again. This was evoked when Lord Lonsdale made a claim for £12,904 as the aqueduct to take the Thirlmere water south passed through lands over which he had Manorial Rights. He also claimed compensation for the stone taken out of the tunnel and used for concrete making.

Although he employed the same solicitors as the Countess, the Award of the Umpire on 24th December 1894 was £1991 a difference of £10,913.

Before that date, when the new dam had been formally opened and blessed by those who in 1877 were protesting against the scheme, Parson Lawson, Vicar of Wythburn, would be at rest, having ministered and inspired love and respect in circumstances far removed from those of his early years in the Thirlmere valley.

For a short time, little changed. Lyddy Hinde went on brewing her tea in the farm that now belonged to Manchester until she died in 1893, but many of parson Lawson's parishioners must have tended the sheep and worked the fields with heavy hearts knowing that nothing would ever be quite the same again.

In the 1880's Huts were erected at Legberthwaite, Armboth and Wythburn and an extra schoolroom built at Legberthwaite. A hospital was set up at Armboth and reading and recreation rooms provided at Armboth and Legberthwaite. When snow and frost made living and working arduous a soup kitchen was set up and daily meals given free to all. Thousands of workmen and their families had their homes in the huts and in the houses and farms of Parson Lawson's parish. An ageing man he had to cope with the toll that the operations took of young lives. In 1888 he entered in the Wythburn registers the burial of George Thorneycroft aged 18 of Dunmail Raise Huts and John Roberts aged 25, killed in the tunnel. There were others from Waterhead and Wythburn huts but there were also baptisms of children born to the worker's wives. Over eighty years old himself, the last entry that he made in his parish registers was a sad one, a local child, Mary Birkett died at just eight years old.

He must have been pleased to know how much his life and work in Wythburn had been appreciated. When repairs were being made to the west end of the church in 1888, Henry Holliday a follower of Burne-Jones was commissioned to provide new stained glass windows.

The three lancet windows in rich red and blues show a red-robed king with orb and sceptre flanked by Saint Cuthbert, with the head of Saint Oswald, and Saint Herbert. Along the base of the windows are the words:

Erected to Rev. B. R. Lawson.
A token of love and esteem from many friends and parishioners.
August 1888 Glory to God.

There must have been an upsurge of affection for the old parson who had worked and played, laughed and cried, brought up his children and taught others amongst the people of Wythburn through almost forty years. They knew that the years in front of him must be few and that with his passing would go the old life in the Vale of Thirlmere and all their yesterdays.

The foundation stone of the great embankment that was to hold back the waters was laid in August 1890 but Parson Lawson did not live to see the risen lake when the structure was completed.

Basil Ranaldson Lawson,
1807 - 1892.

Basil Ranaldson Lawson (Bazzy) born 1848.
About to depart for the City of London.

Henrietta Ada Lawson born 1855.

Fanny Eliza Lawson
born 1857.

The following paragraph appeared in the Westmorland Gazette for June 11th 1892.

Very many of my readers will regret to learn that the Rev. Basil Lawson the Vicar of Wythburn's modest house of prayer' passed away at the vicarage of that beautiful valley on Wednesday at the good age of 84 (86?) years. The last time I saw Mr. Lawson was at Grasmere sports about seven years ago. He was then feeble and had to lean on the willing arm of his daughter. Mr. Lawson was educated at Heversham school, of which parish his father the Rev. Dr. Lawson was the vicar for many years. Mr. Basil Lawson held the living at Wythburn for 41 years and was a great favourite with everybody. Always fond of athletic sports t'parson was a welcome guest at every function of the changing seasons whether Laying outs or clippings. Beyond and above all these Mr. Lawson was a warm hearted father of his flock in the best sense and the kindly personality of Basil Lawsons will linger as a sweet savour in the memory of his parishioners and friends.

THE FAMILY MAN.

The 'warm hearted father of his flock' was truly father to a son and three daughters. They would grow up to know him as a mature man since he was around forty when son 'Bazzy', also Basil Ranaldson Lawson was born in Leicestershire, in 1848. Elizabeth Ann, the mother of all the children was much younger than her husband, being twenty four when Bazzy was baptised. Ellen Elizabeth, the daughter of the diary years was born at Armboth in 1852, Henrietta Ada at Wheyfold in 1855 and the youngest girl, Fanny Eliza followed in 1857.

The family was complete but as with so many a century and a half ago the young mother did not survive to see them out of childhood. Elizabeth Ann Lawson was buried at Saint John's in the Vale in 1862 with the service taken by John Taylor, a curate colleague of the Wythburn Parson.

The new parsonage was in the process of building and a Vicar, with a growing family needs a wife. In 1865 Basil R. Lawson, widower married Ann Clewly, widow of a doctor, and family life was restored. The young Basil was probably away at school by this time. (A later photograph in the family album shows him about to depart to the City of London.) He reappears in the Wythburn registers when he came home so that the Reverend Lawson might baptise his first grandchild. The entry reads:- 1874, June 18th. Fanny Lucy daughter of Basil Ranaldson Lawson and Mary Crowe. Father's occupation is given as 'gentleman' of Brixton, Surrey. Enquiries there have failed to yield any information but W. G. Collingwood in the Lake Counties first published in 1902 has the following interesting paragraph.

"Another scrap of Wythburn wit is given me by a native of the dale, known to many under his pen-name of Rowland Thirlmere. He met a late vicar's son who had been in a stockjobber's office. An old farmer came up, with

'Eh Mr.B--, so you're back again. And whey may ye be dewin?'

'What do you think?'

'O, happen you're a beast (cattle) jobber?'

'No, I'm a jobber in STOCK - which, in one sense, is the same thing!'"

1888 Windows in West End, Wythburn.

Miss Ada Hallam, aged 95, Easter Sunday 1989.

Memorial Window, Wythburn.

Grave of Rev. B. R. Lawson.

This can only have been 'Bazzy'.

Rowland Thirlmere was the pen-name of John Walker (1861-1932) a descendent of Robert Walker, the 18th century Vicar of Seathwaite who features in William Wordsworth's River Duddon series of sonnets. (XVIII) and whom H.A.L Rice described as 'Wonderful Walker' in Lake Country Portraits.

John Walker's father was a friend of the Reverend Basil Lawson, who educated the boy at Wythburn alongside his own younger children. Fanny Lawson told her daughter Ada Hallam that Johnnie was a bright boy and that when she and her sister, Henrietta were slow in learning, their short tempered father often told them that Johnnie would have done the work in half the time.

At eighteen John Walker went into an office in Bury, Lancs. He studied languages and read widely. Later he travelled abroad before settling in the London area from where he renewed acquaintance with his childhood friend, Fanny in her late husband's parish in Suffolk.

Between 1898 and 1930 eight volumes of poetry and two of prose were published as well as a political work 'The Clash of Empires' in 1907, forecasting the coming of the Great War in 1914. A collected edition of his poems was published posthumously in 1934. The preface of this volume describing him as enjoying 'poetry, music, good fellowship and good fare' and never losing his love of the countryside and the beauties of the slopes of Helvellyn in Spring. These characteristics must have been implanted by his tutor, Reverend Lawson, and the people and places where he spent his childhood. Two poems 'Millennial Fire' and 'The Armboth Spruce' seem to encapsulate his feelings for the Vale of Thirlmere from whence he took his literary name.

In 1871, according to the Census returns, the Vicar was surrounded by petticoat rule at the Wythburn Vicarage. The three daughters with his wife, Ann, a border, Evangeline Allison aged fourteen and a domestic servant were all there. Ellen was eighteen and beyond this I have no trace of her. Henrietta Ada, who was then fourteen, was married from Wythburn in 1882 to John Watson Nelson a widower of Langwathby. They lived at Eden Bank, a warm red sandstone house west of the village green and there a year or so later the Reverend Lawson's first, possibly his only grandson was born. Thomas Basil Nelson would certainly be taken to visit his elderly grandfather who died when the boy was nine. However, he grew to be a man who might have delighted Parson Lawson's heart and may well have inherited some of the traits of his character. Cumberland and Westmorland's Who's Who for 1937:- 'Thomas Basil Nelson. J.P.,B.A. Stratheden, Langwathby. b.1883 Ed. Sedbergh & Christ's College Cambridge. m.1912 Dorothy Elaine Sanderson. Served during the Great War - Voluntary Ambulance Driver. Verdun 1916 then Lieutenant R.A.F. Master Ullswater Foxhounds 1931-35. Recreations. Shooting, Hunting, Golf'.

When John Watson Nelson died Thomas Basil inherited all his household furniture, plate books, pictures and household effects; all watches, jewellery, guns and articles of personal use; all horses; carriages, stable furniture, farm and garden implements and stock and all real estate to use during his lifetime. 'T.B.', as he was known in his village, was clearly a man of substance and an administrator of considerable lands. He built the Village Hall and is remembered as a wise landlord and a benefactor in Langwathby.

* In Appendix. Poems, Millennial Fire dedicated to W.G. Collingwood and The Armboth Spruce.

Wythburn Church about 1870 before addition of the chancel in 1872.

Thirlmere, looking north.
Armboth fields reaching to the old bridge across the lake.

The passing years and the sadness of change drained the parson's strength. To join his wife, Ann, and his youngest daughter, Fanny, at the Vicarage and to take over the duties of the parish, there came a curate from Ireland. He served the Wythburn parish during the last two years of Parson Lawson's life and captured the heart of his daughter. William Edward Hallam entered the record of the burial of Basil Ranaldson Lawson in Wythburn parish registers on June 12th 1892

Parson Lawson left all his possessions to be shared equally by his wife and daughter, Fanny Eliza. The gross value of his personal estate was £75.12.6d. He had served God, not Mammon.

The Reverend Hallam and Fanny had their future in hand. The Westmorland Gazette printed the notice of their marriage, within a few weeks of Parson Lawson's death, 'August 15th at Wythburn Church by the Rev. Robt Vaughan, Vicar of Saint John's in the Vale, Keswick. Rev. William Edward Hallam eldest son of the Rev. Cannon Hallam M.A., Rector of Tomb, Diocese of Ferns, County Wexford to Fanny youngest daughter of the late Rev. Basil Ranaldson Lawson, Vicar of Wythburn, Cumberland.'

A new Vicar was appointed to Wythburn, Reverend Winfried des Voeux Hill, and the Rev. Hallam and his wife with her stepmother, Ann Lawson moved on to Newent in Gloucester where a daughter was born and baptised with the family names of Ada Ranaldson. In 1896 there was a move to Barnardiston Rectory in Suffolk where he was Rector until his death in 1915. Fanny Hallam kept up her links with Cumberland and in particular with the son of 'Countess' Ossalinsky. Vladimir Boris Jackson, married Sarah Wilkinson Hardy, a butcher's daughter from Shoulthwaite and never assumed any title. They were firm friends of the Lawsons at Wythburn Vicarage and Vladimir escorted Fanny to the altar when she married the Rev. Hallam. Vladimir's daughter, Ethel, and Fanny's daughter became friends and remained so until Ethel's death at her home, Nether Place in Keswick in 1949.

Ada Ranaldson Hallam, now aged ninety five still lives in her father's parish in Suffolk. She regrets that the family name of Lawson has died out from her very clerical family. Thomas Nelson had no children and Basil Lawson, two daughters, one grandson and one grandaughter. If Parson Lawson has any other descendants it will be from their line, or from Ellen who may have married away from Cumbria.

1894-1989

The Thirlmere that Parson Lawson knew and loved is far beyond any living memory and while there may be many who decried Manchester's policy of destruction of most of the buildings on the lake verge, the planting of conifers and the exclusion of the public from the shores of the reservoir, there can be no doubt that we have gained in some ways. At the ceremonies in 1894 marking the completion of nearly twenty years of work, great pride and noble sentiments were expressed. Alderman Sir Bodsin T. Leech said that the citizens of Manchester had been placed in possession of 11 000 acres of land and had set an example to the country in the nationalising or municipalising of land: Sir John Harwood maintained that the undertaking was an unspeakable gain to the district and Canon Rawnsley prayed for the blessing on the love that inspired the design, the wisdom that planned and oversaw and the patience that endured to it's completion. He remembered 'those who put their hand to this work', 'those who rejoiced in their toiling and in the sweat of their brow found bread' and 'those who gave up their lives to give this gift of gathered waters to many generations'.

At lunch in the temporary schoolroom at Bridge End, Canon Rawnsley proposed a toast to Manchester Waterworks Committee hoping that the local authorities could -'trust Manchester in the future to help them in the battle for preserving the beauty of this Land of the Lakes'.

So for many years it can be asserted that Manchester carried out it's stewardship of the valley thoroughly and well. After the Second World War the administration passed to the North West Water Authority, who with improved water treatment methods were able to allow once again public access to certain parts of the lake. Some of the Armboth trees matured untouched and were seen and appreciated once more, including a remarkable beech with two distinctly different types of leaves and a huge Monkey Puzzle tree.

During the drought of 1984, the old roads and the foundations of the cottages at Bank and the City emerged for the first time in fifty years. The stumps of drowned willows that fringed the lower meadows were once again warmed by a long forgotten sun. Descendants of those who walked there years ago went to look and imagine the places their forefathers knew but the rains came, the reservoirs refilled and the strange brooding sadness of Thirlmere returned. At night there is no light to be seen after leaving Grasmere over Dunmail Raise and winding beside the moonlight reflecting water until one dips down to the Kings Head Hotel at Thirlspot.

There are times, however when the valley is as alive and thronged with visitors, walkers, hunters and fishermen as it ever was but they do not stay. They depart and the silence returns. All the land that Manchester Corporation bought is now administered by the North West Water Authority and there are proposals that this and similar large undertakings should be 'Privatised'. Should this happen, the land could be sold piecemeal to private owners and could drastically alter its use. Already Dalehead Hall is a country house hotel and the Kings Head has an owner with plans for tourist orientated development. Those who earn their living by sheep farming, though few, are apprehensive about their future. Once more the small men, who love the place as it is will oppose the greater men whose interests are different from theirs. May Wythburn Chapel still stand as witness of eternal values and a reminder of stability in a changing world. The little church, the little book and the words of Basil Ranaldson Lawson are the outward and visible signs that reach across the years giving, like the beam of light piecing the clouds, a glimpse of inward and spiritual grace.

THE ARMBOTH SPRUCE

THIS lofty spruce, that stands in lordship o'er the valley
Above the tawny pastures awakening in the spring,
Spake to my heart a word that made old memories rally,—
Seized me and bade me pause to hear its tenant sing.

Bending towards their lord, and offering gold, the larches
Whisper their allegiance, and all the throbbing air
Quickens now to feed him with light of olden Marches—
The sheen of sunny noons that fell on golden hair.

Below his rocky throne, and bowing to the waters
A chestnut tree is flaunting her jewelled points of gold,
And in the old year's garth her daffodils' shy daughters
Gleam golden, and the snow is as a story told:

High in storm and sunshine this tree has viewed the sorrows—
The gradual fair mutations—of twice three hundred years,
And, green in whitest frost, has imaged hopeful morrows
Of nested love, and promised spring in time of tears.

There—so oft beholding our dalesmen fathers weeping
Upon the ancient highway behind the silent tread
Of those whom Death had sought at his drear time of reaping—
The giant spruce would wave his dusky pall o'erhead.

O thou aspiring peak, what murmur art thou making?
That exquisite susurrus is surely meant to be
Charged with hopeful meaning, to comfort spirits aching
For what the Spring unfolds not,—what they cannot see.

A chaffinch seeks thy shadow,—clear his sudden singing
Touches the heart; its music blends to utter this:
Heaven is Past and Present;—our yesterdays are clinging
Unto the young Day's robe, where every Eden is.

Death blows away the blossom, but Life at length replaces
Its light: in gloomiest hours the unseen joys are clear:
Behold the leafless boughs, but mark the wide blue spaces,
The amethyst and amber of visions far and near!

O mighty spruce, in thee I hear a voice that thrills me
With visions of strange glory;—aloft the buzzards mew;
To them my spirit hastes in the wild joy that fills me
To float in skies of Thought suffused with primal blue.

Armboth, *Easter Sunday, 1907.*

MILLENNIAL FIRE

To W. G. Collingwood.

THE blue flame flits across the peat
  Now that the lamp has gone;
The old-world darkness is more sweet
  Than daylight full of sun.

Our shepherd hosts are sleepy; we
  Being wakeful, linger here
In scented dusk, where memory
  Makes dead men reappear.

The turves, close-piled within the garth,—
  Heaped where stout farmers laid
The fuel for their Saxon hearth,—
  Drip in the yews' black shade.

Those trees have lasted like this fire
  Lit when young Ethelred
Was king,—which none has let expire,
  Nor living folk nor dead.

This hearthstone for a thousand years
  Has never once been cold:
The lambent flame of it still cheers
  The old race as of old.

And rarer fire burns steadfastly
  Here, in the yeoman mind,
Proud of an ancient pedigree
  Through pure descent refined.

We see it flash in mountain eyes,
  Feel it in each rough hand—
That deathless warmth from which uprise
  The glories of our land.

BIBLIOGRAPHY.

Bradley A. G.	Highways and Byways in the Lake District. 1919
Burgess J.	Christians in Cumbria. 1982
Caruthers J.	Around Lakeland Hills. 1976
Collingwood W. G.	The Lake Counties. Rev. ed. 1933
Dickinson W.	Cumbriana. 1876
Hudleston C. R. and Boumphrey R.S.	Cumberland Families and Heraldry. 1978
Lefebure M.	Cumberland Heritage. 1970
McFadzean A.	Wythburn Mine. 1987
Marshall J. D.	Old Lakeland. 1971
Marshall J. D. and Walton J. K.	The Lake Counties from 1830 - mid twentieth century. 1981
Martineau H.	Guide to the Lakes. 1855
Millward R. and Robinson A.	The Lake District. 1970
Nicholson N.	The Lakers. 1955
Rice H. A. L.	Lake Country Portraits. 1967
Richardson J.	Cummerland Talk. 1st series. 2nd ed. 1886
Skelton W. C.	Reminiscences of Joe Bowman and the Ullswater Foxhounds. 1921
Trevelyn G. M.	Illustrated English Social History. 1959
Widdup H. L.	The Story of Christianity in Cumbria. 1981
Wilson H.	A Prime Minister on Prime Ministers. 1977
Williams L. A.	Road Transport in Cumbria in the 19th Century. 1975
Wordsworth W.	A Guide through the district of the Lakes of Northern England. 5th ed. 1835

Main directories used were:-	Parson and White, Cumberland and Westmorland 1929.
	Mannix and Whellan, Cumberland 1847
	Mannix & Co. Westmorland 1851.
	Bulmer & Co. Cumberland 1884

POSTSCRIPT

The summer of 1989 was dry and very warm with demand for and use of water greater than ever before. Thirlmere was about 20ft. above the original water surface level, at the shore line reached by the first stage of flooding after the dam was built. The full capacity of the reservoir made possible by the second stage of flooding is thirty feet above that.

Ruined walls were visible clearly marking the boundaries of fields at Waterhead and Armboth. Within days sprouting tiny plants transformed silt into verdure and it was almost possible to imagine the valley of a century ago.

Once again the remains of 'The City' were exposed and pilgrims made their way down by Dob Gill to view the date 1871 picked out in white stones before someone's front door. They were laid only a few years before that person (probably a Birkett) knew that he would have to abandon his house. Travellers, few and curious, once more passed along the road outside the 'Cherry Tree' and walked down the lane from Armboth to the farmhouse at Nether Place.

These demolished buildings are stark and sterile unlike those of Bank the Nag's Head and (Hollin) Brow which being above the usual water line nature has covered with a decent shroud of mosses, grass and shrubbery.

Always there are people visiting the Vale of Thirlmere for the first time, knowing nothing of its past. I hope that they, as well as many who are familiar with and love the area may find something of interest in this booklet.

M.A.

Selective Index